# GREAT BOWLS OF FIRE

# ALSO BY JAY SOLOMON

*Seven Pillars of Health: Nutritional Secrets for Good Health and Long Life*

*Vegetarian Times' Lowfat and Fast Mexican Cookbook*

*Vegetarian Times' Vegetarian Entertaining*

*Vegetarian Times' Lowfat and Fast Pasta Cookbook (coauthor)*

*Lean Bean Cuisine*

*Vegetarian Rice Cuisine*

*Vegetarian Soup Cuisine*

*The Global Vegetarian: Adventures in a Meatless Kitchen*

*A Taste of the Tropics*

*Global Grilling*

*Chutneys, Relishes, and Table Sauces*

JAY SOLOMON

# Great Bowls
# of Fire

THE WORLD'S SPICIEST
SOUPS, CHILIES,
STEWS, AND HOT POTS

PRIMA PUBLISHING

PRIMA PUBLISHING and colophon are registered trademarks of Prima Communications, Inc.

Library of Congress Cataloging-in-Publication Data
Solomon, Jay.
Great bowls of fire: the World's spiciest soups, chilies, stews, and hot pots / Jay Solomon.
p.   cm.
Includes index.
ISBN 0-7615-0927-5
1. Soups. 2. Cookery (Hot peppers) 3. Spices. I. Title.
TX757.5632 1997
641.8'.3—dc21                        97-25440
CIP

97  98  99  00  01  BB  10  9  8  7  6  5  4  3  2  1
Printed in the United States of America

### How to Order

Single copies may be ordered from Prima Publishing, P.O. Box 1260BK, Rocklin, CA 95677;
telephone (916) 632-4400. Quantity discounts are also available. On your letterhead,
include information concerning the intended use of the books
and the number of books you wish to purchase.

**Visit us online at www.primapublishing.com**

*To my cousins*
*Zachary Noggle*
*and Alena Shalaby*

# Contents

# Acknowledgments

---

As THIS IS my twelfth book, I would like to recognize the culinary professionals and pioneering authors who have introduced me (and countless others) to the joys of hot-and-spicy cuisine.

★ Paul Prudhomme, author of *Chef Paul Prudhomme's Louisiana Kitchen*, the classic Cajun cookbook that enthralled me as a young chef and triggered my interest in fervently spiced foods.

★ Chris Schlesinger and John Willoughby, authors of *The Thrill of the Grill*, a trailblazing, pleasure-filled cookbook that incited me to riot and rebel against the staid flavors of the status quo.

★ Mark Miller and John Harrison, authors of *The Great Chile Book*, the definitive guide to the world's most popular chili peppers (the book is lavishly accompanied by beautiful photographs).

★ Jean Andrews, author of *Peppers: The Domesticated Capsicums*, a wonderfully illustrated (and exhaustively researched) text that illuminates the culinary usage and historical, cultural, and botanical background of chili peppers.

★ Dave DeWitt, the founding editor of *Chile Pepper* magazine, prolific author, and avid booster of all things hot and spicy.

★ Chef Dean Fearing, author of *The Mansion on Turtle Creek Cookbook*, a trendsetting book that inspired a new generation of chefs to explore the dynamic elements of Southwestern cuisine.

★ Restaurateurs Roger Harman, Duane Ball, and the staff at the Palladium Restaurant and Bar in Philadelphia, my long-time sponsors at "The Book and The Cook" celebration, an annual culinary collaboration between cookbook authors and restaurateurs.

★ Frieda's Finest, suppliers of exotic produce and a dizzying array of chili peppers, many of which I used throughout this book.

I also wish to thank Georgia Hughes and Jennifer Fox, my editors at Prima Publishing, who have enthusiastically (and patiently) supported my writing endeavors. Additionally, the Solomons, the Robins, and a cadre of friends near and far have supported and promoted my cookbooks throughout the years.

Finally, I owe a tremendous debt of gratitude to my wonderful wife, Emily, my lifelong partner in the pursuit of the piquant, the pungent, and the spicy-hot.

# Introduction

---

BLAZING, BURNING, BLISTERING, flaming. To scorch, to sear, to sizzle, to torch. Wonderfully pungent, bordering on volcanic, terrifically torrid. A blaze of glory, a wildfire raging, bells and whistles, sirens wailing. Pow—right in the kisser! Hotter than hell.

These are the words and phrases I use to describe my favorite foods. I have a penchant for the piquant, a fondness for the fiery, a weakness for the wickedly hot. Chili peppers make my day; hot sauces make me smile. My garden overflows with colorful jalapeños, cayennes, serranos, and habaneros. There is a fresh supply of peppers in my refrigerator at all times, ready for action. Lest there ever be a shortage, the freezer is full of them. The mild and the bland are to be loathed and deplored. I love all things hot. Chili peppers adorn my family crest.

I am not alone in my quest for fire and spice. Kitchens across the country beckon with simmering cauldrons of spicy soups, chilies, stews, and hot pots. From family kitchens and fancy restaurants to neighborhood taverns and festive gatherings, tables are set with steaming tureens and tempting bowls. These are the days of the hot, the spicy, and the boldly flavored. It is a glorious time to be alive.

In this exuberant spirit comes *Great Bowls of Fire,* a hit parade of the world's spiciest one-pot wonders. From Wild Mushroom and Chicken Gumbo, Sante Fe Black Bean Soup, and Fiery Chicken Congo to Pacific Noodle Soup and Jamaican Chicken Curry, here is a carnival of recipes that promise to excite your appetite and entice your palate. Spicy delights such as Red Pepper Vichyssoise, Triple Chili Ratatouille, and Bourbon Street Jambalaya will make your taste buds sing and dance and send your pulse racing.

Chili peppers are the heroes of hot-and-spicy cuisine, and naturally, they are the stars of this book. The pungent pods transform the mundane into the magnificent, reinvigorate the bland, rescue the listless, and convert the mild to wild. The diverse family of chili peppers includes versatile jalapeños, searing serranos, curvy poblanos, symphonic New Mexicos, rustic anchos, and scorching Scotch bonnets. In addition to chilies galore—fresh, dried, ground, and pickled—the piquant arsenal includes a bounty of garden herbs, aromatic spices, bottled hot sauces, and potent spice pastes.

Although not every recipe in *Great Bowls of Fire* is an inferno waiting to engulf your mouth, all the meals are spiced with gusto and verve. Often, a kind of culinary harmony is achieved, a clever balancing of tastes, textures, and colors. Sometimes the heat sneaks up on you without warning, like a surprise party. Other times, the mouth glows warmly in the dark, a fireplace of savory sensations; the lips tingle. Occasionally, records are shattered, rules are broken; the spice pedal is pushed to the floor, the throttle is at full-tilt, and a turbocharged heat is unleashed. To pepper aficionados, this is pure bliss.

The recipes in *Great Bowls of Fire* hail from every corner of the globe. From the sunny American Southwest come black bean soup, posole, and hearty harvest stews. Creole and Cajun cooking from Louisiana gives forth myriad gumbos, jambalayas, and down-home one-pot dishes. Of course, there are plenty of inviting variations of down-home chili ("a bowl of red"), the pride of Texas and a venerated culinary icon.

Mexican fare sparkles with boisterous bean soups, fragrant sopas, and spicy pilafs. The balmy Caribbean offers a mosaic of spicy delights such as pepperpot, red pea soup, sancocho, conch and seafood chowders, and pumpkin bisque. Expansive South America is home to smoky black bean feijoada, porotos granados, wholesome locro, and other satisfying one-pot dishes.

This hall of fame for flame includes recipes from the world's spice capital, India, home of fragrant curries, dals, mulligatawnys, and sambars. Pan-African recipes feature traditional and improvised versions of groundnut stews, festive jollof rice, and tagines. The Pacific Rim inspires bountiful recipes for tempting Thai curries, alluring noodle soups, and Asian firepots.

Welcome to *Great Bowls of Fire*, a celebration of fierce flavors and adventurous tastes. Prepare your senses for an amusement park of thrilling one-pot dishes served in bowls brimming with anticipation. Get ready to indulge in the sizzling and the sublime, fire up the stove, stoke up your appetite, and let the fireworks begin!

# The Piquant Pantry

THROUGHOUT THIS BOOK, a cornucopia of fresh and dried chili peppers provide the fireworks—and serve as culinary inspiration as well. A battalion of hot sauces and spice pastes are deployed for instant boosts of intense flavors. A spice rack of seasonings offers balance and depth to simmering pots, while garden herbs contribute refreshing nuances. Indeed, the pursuit of the piquant is a team approach.

## A Guide to Chili Peppers

Hundreds of varieties of chili peppers are grown around the world, from the versatile jalapeño and curvy green poblano to the sleek New Mexico chili and wild-looking Scotch bonnet pepper. Chilies come in all shapes, colors, sizes, and levels of heat. The realm of chili peppers is diverse, alluring, and rarely boring.

What makes a chili pepper hot? The heat of a chili pepper is derived from a natural plant compound known as capsaicin. Although it has no flavor, color, or smell, capsaicin causes a burning sensation when it enters the mouth or touches the lips. The amount of capsaicin in a chili pepper determines the level of heat. For example, a fiery Scotch bonnet pepper contains a mother lode of capsaicin, while a sweet bell pepper is virtually capsaicin-free. Simply put, capsaicin puts the *hot* into the chili pepper.

Although capsaicin is spread unevenly throughout the pepper, it is highly concentrated in the seeds and the membranes connecting the seeds to the chili's inside walls. By removing and discarding the seeds before cooking, a smoother distribution of heat can be achieved. (This explains why most recipes call for removing the seeds of the chili prior to cooking.)

So why do so many peoples of the world nurture a penchant for the piquant? For starters, a taste of pepper and spice provides culinary excitement and adventurous flavors. A meal will not be dull or nondescript when chili peppers are in the recipe. The difference between bland food and spicy food is the difference between black-and-white and color television, crayon and neon, lightning bug and lightning.

Hyperbole aside, there are scientific theories to explain the palate's desire for the wild instead of the mild. Apparently when capsaicin comes into contact with sensitive nerve endings in the mouth and nose, pain receptors ignite a chain of chemical reactions. A message makes a beeline to the brain, which then triggers the release of natural painkilling chemicals called endorphins. In fact, not only do endorphins kill pain, but they also contain pleasure-producing properties. With capsaicin acting as the catalyst, the burning sensation associated with hot food is followed by a sense of pleasure and well-being brought on by endorphins, the body's natural painkillers. Endorphins have been likened to natural opiates manufactured by the body.

The thrill-and-chill syndrome derived from hot-and-spicy food is similar to riding a roller coaster. The fear and panic associated with a roller coaster swerving and plummeting to earth is directly followed by a feeling of intense relief as the roller coaster slows. Calm returns, endorphins are deployed, and the body feels reinvigorated, not panicky. The theory goes that this manic cycle of pain and pleasure can also occur during the course of eating an ultra-hot spicy meal.

In addition to producing culinary fireworks, chili peppers are also part of a healthful diet. Chilies are high in beta-carotene and vitamin C and are low in fat, sodium, and calories. There is little need for salt, butter, or cream when vibrant chili peppers are in the recipe. In addition, capsaicin is part of a group of beneficial compounds called phytochemicals (plant chemicals). Like antioxidants and vitamins, phytochemicals help the body defend against a variety of chronic diseases.

## Chili Pepper Etiquette

Here are some tips on buying, storing, and cooking with chili peppers.

★ BUYING Look for chilies that have a taut skin, smooth sheen, and firm stem. Avoid chilies with blemishes, soft spots, wrinkles, or cracks.

★ STORAGE Store fresh chilies in the refrigerator in a plastic bag left slightly open (allowing some air for the peppers to "breathe"). In the refrigerator, moisture is the sworn enemy. If you wash the peppers ahead of time, remember to pat dry the pods using a towel. Like most vegetables and fruits, chili peppers are perishable and should be used within five to seven days. Whole or chopped, chili peppers can also be frozen in airtight bags. Frozen peppers will last up to six months in the freezer.

★ PREPARATION Remove the stem and slit the pod in half lengthwise. Slide a butter knife along the inside of the pepper and remove the seeds (removing the seeds tempers the heat and allows for a smoother heat distribution). The chili pepper is now ready to be minced or sliced.

★ ROASTING A FRESH CHILI Some peppers, such as poblano and New Mexico, are often roasted or grilled prior to using in a recipe. Simply place the pods over an open flame or grill or beneath a broiler for four to six minutes on each side until the skin is charred and puffy. (Pulling out the chili's core and seeds before roasting is optional.) Remove the chilies from the heat and let cool for a few minutes in a colander (some recommend placing the chilies in an airtight container for ten minutes). With a butter knife or your hands, scrape the thin layer of charred skin from the flesh and discard. Remove the remaining seeds and chop or slice the flesh.

★ WARNING: HOT! If you have sensitive skin, it is a good idea to wear plastic or rubber gloves when handling the peppers. Avoid touching any part of your face—the slightest trace of capsaicin transferred from your fingers may cause an unpleasant burning sensation.

★ SPICE RELIEF If your food is too hot, the best strategy for relief is to drink or eat a dairy product, such as milk or yogurt. Dairy products contain a protein (casein) that neutralizes the capsaicin. Drinking ice water, cola, or alcohol doesn't appear to have much effect (and may even intensify the heat). My advice is to compose yourself, wipe your brow, and take another bite.

## An Amusement Park of Flavors: A Glossary of Fresh Chili Peppers

Here is an overview of the world's most popular chili peppers.

**Cayenne chili peppers** are long, narrow chilies with a razor's edge of peppery heat. Although cayennes are often dried and ground into powders and processed into bottled hot sauces, the fresh pods are a favorite ingredient in soups and chili. Green and red cayenne chili peppers are a central flavor in Creole, African, and Indian cuisines.

**Cherry peppers** are a family of small, bulbous peppers with a mild to tingly heat. Cherry peppers have been traced to pre-Columbian times. They are often sold in farmers' markets and well-stocked supermarkets.

**Congo peppers** are the native chili of Trinidad and Tobago and the cousin of Jamaica's Scotch bonnet pepper. Congo peppers give curry dishes, stews, and marinades a bolt of lightning flavor. Congo peppers have also inspired scores of tropical hot sauces.

**Habaneros** are lantern-shaped, colorful pods with a ferocious heat and tropical apricot aroma. Although the name means "from Cuba," habaneros are believed to be indigenous to the Yucatán. Regarded as one of the world's hottest peppers, habaneros are used in salsas, soups, chilies, and bisques and have inspired a cottage industry of bottled hot sauces. Habaneros are closely related to the Scotch bonnet (the peppers are interchangeable in recipes). Orange habaneros are grown commercially in California, Texas, and the Carolinas.

**Hungarian wax peppers,** also called yellow wax hots or chile guero, are yellow to pale-green peppers with the shape of a small contorted banana. They have a medium-to-hot heat range and a subtle citrus flavor. Hungarian wax peppers are in salsas, sauces, soups, and gazpacho. Mild wax peppers are called banana peppers.

**Jalapeños** are thick-fleshed chilies shaped like bullets. Jalapeños range from mild to hot, from dark green to deep red. Perhaps the most versatile pepper in the world, jalapeños are used in salsas, chilies, soups, stews, bean and rice dishes, marinades, and breads. Jalapeños are a mainstay of Mexican and Southwestern cooking (jalapeños are named after Jalapa, a Mexican city). Jalapeños are also available canned, pickled, and smoked and dried (under the name of chipotle).

**New Mexicos** are long, tapered chilies native to the American Southwest. The green and red chilies have a clean, fruity heat and aromatic flavor. New Mexico chilies are always roasted prior to using, to soften the flesh and remove the outer skin. New Mexico chilies can also be dried and are ground into sauces or powders. Do not confuse New Mexico chilies with Anaheim chilies, those long, green-polyester pods with negligible heat.

**Pepperoncinis** are pickled, yellowish-green Italian peppers with a mild bite. Often found on salad bars, pepperoncinis are great for dressings, salads, bean dishes, grain salads, red sauces, and antipasto.

**Poblanos** are large, greenish-purple pods with a contorted anvil shape, sturdy skin, raisiny flavor, and medium-to-hot heat. They are often roasted before using. Poblanos are one of the most popular chilies in Mexico and Southwestern kitchens. Dried poblanos are marketed as ancho chilies.

**Red Fresnos** are similar to red jalapeños but display slightly more heat. Red Fresnos have broad shoulders that taper to a point (jalapeño shoulders have a slouch). The chilies are interchangeable with jalapeños and can be used in salsas, soups, chilies, curries, sauces, and dips.

**Rocatillos,** also called aji dulce, are tiny, multicolored chilies with a pattypan squash shape (they resemble a baby habanero). The chilies have a sweet, citrusy flavor and mild heat. Rocatillos are grown on many Spanish-speaking Caribbean islands, especially Puerto Rico; they are similar to the seasoning pepper enjoyed in Grenada.

**Scotch bonnet peppers** have a turbo, megawatt heat infused with a distinctive floral persona. Native to Jamaica, Scotch bonnets come in a rainbow of colors and sultry curvaceous shapes and are used in jerk sauce, soups, stews, rice-and-pea dishes, and a legion of bottled hot sauces. Their name comes from a resemblance to floppy hats worn by the Scots. Scotch bonnets are also known as country peppers, bonneys, and Bahama mamas. Scotch bonnets are interchangeable with habaneros.

**Seasoning peppers** are neon-colored, curvy pods with a citrusy, sweet flavor and tingly, fleeting heat. Similar to rocatillos, seasoning peppers are popular in Grenada and other Caribbean islands. Unfortunately, they are not yet available in the United States.

**Serranos** are narrow, pointy peppers with a sharp, prickly heat. The pod's canal is dense with seeds, which contribute to its concentrated degree of heat. Serranos come in green, red, and reddish-orange colors and are used in soups, stews, chilies, curries, salsas, and stir-fries. Serranos are interchangeable with hot jalapeños, cayenne chili peppers, and red Fresnos.

**Tabasco peppers** are small, cone-shaped chilies with a rather forceful heat. The pepper is best known for its role in the legendary Louisiana hot sauce, in which the peppers are mashed, fermented, and aged. Tabasco hot sauce is considered to be the world's most popular hot sauce.

## Toasty Aromas and Robust Flavors: A Glossary of Dried Chilies

Recently, the availability of exotic dried chili peppers has skyrocketed. Dried chilies offer a range of spicy nuances and can enliven a variety of soups, chilies, stews, and sauces. Unlike their fresh counterparts, dried chilies have a long shelf life (if properly stored) and can be found in supermarkets throughout the year.

Dried chili peppers require slightly different preparation than fresh chilies. Most chefs prefer to toast dried chilies in an ungreased skillet for a few minutes before adding to a recipe. The dried pods are seared and turned in a sturdy skillet for about two minutes and then covered with simmering hot water and soaked until they are soft, about fifteen to twenty minutes. The chilies can then be added to a soup or stew or pureed with a little soaking liquid and transformed into a thick paste. Another popular method calls for toasting the chilies and grinding them into a spice powder.

Following is a sampling of some popular varieties of dried chili peppers.

**Anchos** are dried green poblano peppers with wide shoulders and a burnt-red, brownish hue. This Mexican favorite has a musky, raisiny flavor and is used in sauces (mole), salsas, and chili-stews. ("Ancho" means "broad" or "wide" in Spanish.)

**Bird peppers,** also known as pequin and chiltepin, are tiny, ovoid peppers with a firecracker (but fleeting) heat. The reddish-orange, berrylike pods have grown wild in the Caribbean for centuries and may have been the chilies Columbus tasted when he stumbled upon America.

**Cascabels** are cherry mahogany–colored chilies with a smoky flavor and a small, bulbous shape. "Casabel" means "rattle" or "jingle" in Spanish (the dried seeds in the pod make a rattling sound when shaken).

**Cayenne chili peppers** are long, thin peppers with an assertive bite. Cayennes are often ground and sold as a powder or processed into bottled hot sauces. Typically, the generic ground red pepper found in stores is made with cayennes. The chili is named after the Cayenne River in French Guiana. Cayenne chili peppers are similar to the chile de arbols grown in Mexico.

**Chile de arbols** are long, narrow pods with a reddish-orange hue, thin skin, and intense heat ("arbol" means "rooster beak"). Arbols are similar to cayenne chili peppers.

**Chipotles** are large jalapeño peppers that have been dried and smoked. Chipotles are available canned in a spicy adobo sauce or air-packed in bags. Soak the air-packed chilies for twenty minutes in warm water before using. Chipotles have a dark brownish-red color, smoky flavor, and piercing heat.

**Guajillos** are long, slender pods with a shiny, reddish-mahogany tint and fruity, almost tart flavor. They are the dried version of the mirasol pepper (which is very hard to find fresh). Guajillos are one of the most popular chilies used in Mexican cooking.

**New Mexicos,** when dried, turn brick-red and develop a tangy, zesty flavor. New Mexico chilies are used in the venerated red chili sauces of Southwestern cuisine as well as chili-stews, posoles, and spicy soups. Dried New Mexico chilies are ground into sauces or powders and are also tied into holiday wreaths (called ristras) and displayed as ornaments.

**Pasillas** are long, dark-brown chilies with a spicy, ancholike flavor. "Pasilla" means "little raisin."

# Liquid Fire: A Glossary of Hot Sauces and Pungent Pastes

The growing enthusiasm for hot-and-spicy fare has inspired a burgeoning market for bottled hot sauces and chili pastes. There is a vast array of hot sauces available, including mild jalapeño sauces, sweet sambals, potent Thai curry pastes, and fiery Scotch bonnet pepper sauces. Instead of reaching for the salt and pepper shakers, more and more cooks are reaching for a bottle of hot sauce or spice paste.

Following is a look at the hot sauces and spice pastes called for throughout this book. Most sauces are found in well-stocked supermarkets and specialty food stores.

**Chili-garlic paste** is a thick, brick-red sauce of red chilies, vinegar, garlic, and Asian spices. Patrons of Asian grocery stores will recognize this sauce by its signature green lids and red-tinted, wide-mouth jars.

**Habanero and Scotch bonnet pepper sauces** contain pureed chilies, vinegar and/or citrus juice, tropical fruits, and occasionally sugar or mustard. The torrid sauces can be red, green, or yellow. A good habanero or Scotch bonnet sauce should have a fruity flavor, blistering heat, and thick (not runny) consistency.

**Harissa** is a brick-red spice paste called for in Moroccan recipes. Cumin, coriander, red chili peppers, and paprika are the core ingredients. Sold in cans or in tubes, harissa is similar to a liquid chili powder.

**Sambal** is an Indonesian chili paste with a flavorful "sweet heat" sensation. Serve this addicting sauce with rice dishes or as a flavoring paste for soups and stews. Sambal is sold in Asian markets and well-stocked supermarkets.

**Tabasco and other Louisiana hot sauces** are piquant, vinegary liquids made from the fermented mash of Tabasco peppers or cayenne chili peppers, depending on the brand. The granddaddy of them all, Tabasco sauce, is perhaps the world's most popular hot sauce. Don't ever run out of it.

**Thai curry paste** is a wet paste of chilies, herbs, and Asian spices typically sold in small cans or plastic pouches. Curry paste, when combined with coconut milk, forms the basis of most Thai curry dishes. The variety of curry pastes include red, yellow, green, panang, and masaman.

## Adding a Touch of Pizzazz: A Glossary of Assertive Spices

While chili peppers supply the thunder and lightning to simmering hot pots, chilies, and stews, dried spices bring essential depth and dimension to the mix. Here is an inventory of the well-stocked spice rack.

**Allspice** is a reddish-brown berry grown in the tropics (many erroneously think of it as a mixture of "all spices"). Allspice's penetrating aroma invokes cinnamon, cloves, and nutmeg. The spice is a central flavor in Caribbean dishes, such as Jamaican jerk barbecue, pumpkin bisque, mango chutney, and rum cake.

**Blackened seasonings,** also called Cajun spices, is an integral flavor of Louisiana cuisine. The spice blend includes cayenne pepper, black pepper, white pepper, paprika, thyme, onion, garlic, and oregano. When choosing a commercial brand, avoid those that list salt as a main ingredient.

**Cayenne pepper** is the fine red powder derived from dried cayenne chili peppers. Also called ground red pepper, cayenne pepper is several times hotter than black pepper. The spice is an integral flavor in Cajun, African, and Indian cuisine and is often used in combination with ground black pepper and/or white pepper. A dash of cayenne can punch up premixed chili powder, curry powder, or blackened seasonings.

**Chili powder,** the spice mixture used in the beloved Tex-Mex chili-stew, includes red pepper, cumin, paprika, oregano, and garlic powder. Commercial brands should have a deep red hue and a musky, peppery aroma. Salt should not be listed as a main ingredient.

**Cumin** is a versatile spice with an earthy, musky aroma and a desert-brown hue. The spice is instrumental in Southwestern salsa, rice pilaf, black bean soup, chili, curry dishes, barbecue rubs, and marinades. Cumin goes well with coriander, oregano, red hot chilies, and other assertive seasonings.

**Curry powder,** the premier spice blend of Indian and Caribbean kitchens, includes a variety of seasonings, such as turmeric, cumin, cloves, coriander, red pepper, ginger, allspice, cinnamon, and mustard. Commercial brands from India or the Caribbean tend to have a stronger, more pronounced flavor than domestic brands. A general rule: To heighten the curry flavor, sear the spices in the pan for a minute or two before adding liquid to the pan.

**Garam masala** is a brownish, aromatic spice blend of cardamom, coriander, cinnamon, cumin, and cloves. Garam masala adds a fragrant dimension to Indian dishes, soups, and curries.

**Nutmeg and mace** both come from the same plant. Nutmeg is a hard, nutlike seed with an oval shape, and mace is the nut's lacy outer covering. The curvy "blades" of mace are removed and ground up separately. Both nutmeg and mace add light flavors to spicy squash soups, chowders, and piña coladas.

**Paprika** is a versatile brick-red spice made from Hungarian peppers that have been dried and finely ground into a powder. A light sprinkling of paprika will perk up potato chowders, chilies, fish soups, and stews.

**Peppercorns** include not just black peppercorns but also white, green, and even red varieties. Black peppercorns are really unripe green berries that have been dried and hardened. When peppercorns are ground or pulverized, a floral, pungent essence is released. The pungency diminishes dramatically after the peppers are ground.

When green berries are freeze-dried, they are sold as green pepper-corns. When green peppercorns are left on the vine to mature, they ripen into red berries. Ripe red berries are soaked, dehydrated, and transformed into white peppercorns. (Pink peppercorns come from an entirely different plant.)

**Red pepper flakes** are dried and coarsely ground shards of hot red chilies. Red pepper flakes are about twice as hot as ground black pepper-corns. Botanically speaking, red pepper flakes are not in the peppercorn family. Red pepper flakes can be used like black pepper when more heat is desired. Remember, a little goes a long way.

**Turmeric** is a vibrant yellowish-orange spice derived from a knobby rhi-zome similar to ginger root. Better known for its color than its flavor, turmeric enlivens squash soups, risottos, curries, and pilafs. Turmeric is often called the "poor man's saffron" because it makes a good substitute for the world's most expensive spice. Turmeric gives table mustard its bright yellow hue.

## Herbal Delights: A Glossary of Garden Herbs

Every chef knows that hot and spicy dishes also rely upon a variety of herbs to bring a sense of balance and refreshing taste to the simmering spice pot. Here are some of the herbs that play a significant role in the pursuit of fiery fare.

**Arugula** is a pale green, oak-shaped leaf with a smart, peppery taste. Also know as rocket or roquette, the Italian herb makes a spicy replacement for basil in pesto and gives salsa a peppery twist. The larger the leaf, the spicier the flavor.

**Basil,** the herb of pesto fame, has a hint of anise, mint, and black pepper. Basil is used in red sauces, tomato-based soups, and Thai curry sauces. Vari-eties include sweet basil, Thai basil, lemon basil, and opal (or purple) basil.

**Cilantro,** also known as Chinese parsley or coriander, has a pungent, cleansing taste (some call it soapy). Cilantro has a physical resemblance to parsley but a taste all its own. Although best known for its role in salsa, cilantro can perk up a range of dishes, including gazpacho, guacamole, curry dishes, Asian soups, and chili-stews.

**Oregano and marjoram** are two herbs with a musky, pine resin fragrance and delicate texture. Widely used in the dried form, the twin herbs are prevalent in Mediterranean, Mexican, and Southwestern dishes.

**Parsley** was chewed as a breath freshener in ancient times. There are two common varieties: curly leaf (which is springy and tightly bunched) and Italian flat leaf (which is loosely bunched and slightly stronger in flavor). The omnipresent herb can enhance almost any bowl.

**Thyme** is an earthy herb with a pungent aroma. The oval petals enliven chowders, squash bisques, bean soups, fish stews, and mushroom soups. Unlike most herbs, fresh thyme retains its flavor during the cooking process. Dried thyme retains most of the flavor of its fresh counterpart.

## Rating the Recipes

Each recipe in *Great Bowls of Fire* is labeled according to its heat factor. Keep the following key in mind when deciding how spicy of a dish you want. And remember, you can always turn down or turn up the heat.

= spicy    = super spicy

= off the scale

# Sizzling Bowls of the American Southwest

IF SOUTHWESTERN COOKING were listed in the dictionary, the words "bold," "exuberant," and "exhilarating" would all be a part of its definition. Southwestern cuisine is a vibrant melting pot of Native American, Spanish, and Mexican cultures, and it is as colorful as it is flavorful. Simmering bowls from the sun-drenched Southwest offer big tastes, bright lights, and loud flavors.

Without a doubt, chili peppers are the heart and soul of Southwestern cooking. The region's most popular pepper is the **New Mexico chili,** a long, slender pod with fruity, cherrylike flavor and mild to hot heat. Fresh red New Mexico chilies are roasted and peeled before using; dried chilies are briefly toasted in a skillet and soaked in water. There is also the **poblano chili,** a dark green pepper with a curvy, bell pepper shape, raisiny flavor, and mellow heat. Dried poblanos, called **ancho chilies,** are also staples of the Southwest pantry.

Of course, there are **jalapeños** galore. The versatile, bullet-shaped chilies are used to enhance soups, stews, sauces, posoles, and salsas. In general, red jalapeños are hotter than green. Also prevalent are fresh and dried cayenne peppers—long, narrow peppers with a prickly heat. Additionally, there is a jalapeño look-alike called **red Fresno,** a bright red chili with broad shoulders and a zippy heat level.

The Southwest pantry includes black beans, pumpkin, winter squash, onions, corn, green peppers, and hominy (also called posole), a dried chewy corn. The pots have plenty of herbs, including cilantro, parsley, oregano, and thyme. The spice rack stretches out to include cumin, coriander, black pepper, cayenne pepper, and ground chili powder.

The great bowls of the Southwestern table include Poblano Chicken Posole, a hearty chili-stew; Sweet Potato–Corn Chowder, a winsome soup; Sante Fe Black Bean Soup; Red Fresno Butternut Bisque; and Succotash Chowder, a satisfying cauldron of lima beans and corn. Savory bowl companions include salsa, guacamole, red chili sauce, tortillas, sopaipillas (a puffy flat bread) and corn bread.

# Succotash Chowder

THIS SAVORY BOWL was inspired by the traditional tandem of lima beans and corn.

| | |
|---|---|
| 1 tablespoon canola oil | 1 can (11 ounces) corn kernels, |
| 1 medium yellow onion, diced | drained |
| 1 red bell pepper, seeded and diced | 2 teaspoons dried oregano |
| 3 cloves garlic, minced | 1 teaspoon ground cumin |
| 2 jalapeño peppers, seeded and | 1 teaspoon paprika |
| minced | ½ teaspoon cayenne pepper |
| 1 cup frozen green lima beans | ½ teaspoon salt |
| 1 medium sweet potato, diced | 1 cup light cream or milk |

IN A LARGE saucepan, heat the oil. Add the onion, bell pepper, garlic, and jalapeños and cook, stirring, for 5 minutes over medium-high heat. Add 4 cups water, the lima beans, and sweet potato and bring to a simmer. Add the corn, oregano, cumin, paprika, cayenne pepper, and salt and cook over medium heat for about 20 minutes, stirring occasionally.

To thicken, ladle 2 cups of the chowder into a food processor fitted with a steel blade or into a blender and process until pureed, about 5 seconds. Return to the pan and stir in the cream. Return the chowder to a gentle simmer over medium-low heat.

Ladle the chowder into bowls and serve with warm flour tortillas.

YIELD: 6 SERVINGS

# Sweet Potato—Corn Chowder

PAPRIKA, OREGANO, AND cumin imbue this chowder with appealing flavors and aromas. The mighty jalapeños provide a nice kick.

For a slightly different chowder, replace the sweet potato with an exotic potato. Try Yukon Gold potatoes, blue potatoes, or fingerlings.

1 tablespoon canola oil

1 medium yellow onion, diced

1 red bell pepper, seeded and diced

2 stalks celery, chopped

3 or 4 cloves garlic, minced

2 jalapeño peppers, seeded and
    minced

5 cups water or vegetable broth

1 large sweet potato, diced

2 teaspoons dried oregano

2 teaspoons paprika

1½ teaspoons ground cumin

½ teaspoon black pepper

½ teaspoon salt

1 can (15 ounces) corn kernels,
    drained

1 cup light cream or milk

3 or 4 scallions, chopped

2 tablespoons chopped fresh cilantro
    (optional)

IN A LARGE saucepan, heat the oil. Add the onion, bell pepper, celery, garlic, and jalapeño peppers and cook, stirring, for about 6 minutes over medium-high heat. Add the water, sweet potato, oregano, paprika, cumin, black pepper, and salt and bring to a simmer. Cook over medium heat for 10 minutes, stirring occasionally. Add the corn and cook until the sweet potato is tender, about 10 minutes more, stirring occasionally.

Stir in the cream, scallions, and optional cilantro and return to a simmer. Remove from the heat and let stand for 5 minutes. To thicken, ladle about 2 cups of the soup into a blender or food processor fitted with a steel blade and puree until smooth, about 5 seconds. Return the pureed soup to the pan.

Ladle the chowder into bowls and serve at once with warm homemade corn bread.

YIELD: 6 SERVINGS

### Some Like It Hotter

ADD A FEW TEASPOONS OF
BOTTLED HOT SAUCE
INTO THE CHOWDER JUST
BEFORE SERVING.

# Sante Fe Black Bean Soup

THIS SOOTHING, SATISFYING black bean soup can lift one's spirits on a cold, bleak day. Remember, dried beans should always be soaked in plenty of water before cooking; after draining, cook the beans in fresh water.

1½ cups dried black beans, soaked
    overnight and drained

1 tablespoon canola oil

1 large yellow onion, diced

1 red bell pepper, seeded and diced

1 large stalk celery, chopped

3 or 4 cloves garlic, minced

1 or 2 jalapeño peppers, seeded and
    minced

2 medium carrots, peeled and diced

1 tablespoon dried oregano

1½ teaspoons ground cumin

1 teaspoon ground coriander

1 teaspoon dried thyme

1 teaspoon salt

½ teaspoon black pepper

½ cup canned crushed tomatoes

¼ cup chopped fresh parsley

2 tablespoons chopped fresh
    cilantro

IN A MEDIUM saucepan, combine the beans and 6 cups water and bring to a simmer. Cook over medium-low heat until tender, about 1½ hours. Drain the beans, reserving 4 cups of the cooking liquid.

In a large saucepan, heat the oil. Add the onion, bell pepper, celery, garlic, and jalapeño and cook, stirring, for 5 minutes over medium heat. Add the beans, cooking liquid, carrots, oregano, cumin, coriander, thyme, salt, and black pepper and bring to a simmer. Cook for about 15 minutes over medium heat, stirring occasionally.

Stir in the crushed tomatoes, parsley, and cilantro and cook for 5 to 10 minutes more, stirring occasionally. Remove from the heat and let stand for 5 minutes. For a thicker soup, ladle half of the soup into a blender or food processor fitted with a steel blade and puree until smooth, about 5 seconds. Return the pureed soup to the pan.

Ladle the soup into bowls. Serve with warm corn bread.

YIELD: 6 SERVINGS

✗ *Spice Advice*

ADD A SPOON OF SOUR CREAM
OR PLAIN YOGURT TO THE
BOWLS BEFORE SERVING.

# Poblano and Crayfish Chowder

POBLANO CHILIES LEND an enticing Southwestern flavor to this seafood chowder.

2 or 3 poblano chilies, cored and
    seeded

1 tablespoon canola oil

1 medium yellow onion, diced

1 red bell pepper, seeded and diced

2 stalks celery, chopped

3 or 4 cloves garlic, minced

1 large sweet potato, diced

2 teaspoons dried oregano

1½ teaspoons paprika

1 teaspoon dried thyme

½ teaspoon salt

½ teaspoon black pepper

½ pound precooked crayfish meat or
    lump crab meat, cartilage
    removed (thawed, if frozen)

1 can (11 ounces) corn kernels, drained

1 cup light cream or milk

To ROAST THE poblanos, place them over a hot grill or beneath a pre-heated broiler for 4 to 5 minutes on each side until the skin is charred. Remove from the heat and let cool for a few minutes. Using a butter knife, peel off the charred skin. Chop the flesh.

In a large saucepan, heat the oil. Add the onion, bell pepper, celery, and garlic and cook, stirring, for about 6 minutes over medium-high heat. Add the roasted chilies, 4 cups water, the sweet potato, oregano, paprika, thyme, salt, and black pepper and bring to a simmer. Cook over medium heat for 10 minutes. Stir in the crayfish and corn and return to a simmer. Cook for about 10 minutes more, stirring occasionally.

Stir in the cream and return to a gentle simmer. To thicken, ladle about 2 cups of the chowder into a food processor fitted with a steel blade or into a blender and puree until smooth, about 5 seconds. Return the pureed soup to the pan.

Ladle the chowder into bowls and serve at once.

YIELD: 6 SERVINGS

✗ *Spice Advice*

ADD 2 OR 3 TABLESPOONS

OF CHOPPED HERBS,

SUCH AS CILANTRO OR CHIVES,

TO THE CHOWDER

JUST BEFORE SERVING.

# Sunset Potato Bisque

SWEET AND HOT peppers, along with cumin and cilantro, form a striking combination of flavors and colors.

| | |
|---|---|
| 1 tablespoon canola oil | 4 cups diced sweet potatoes |
| 1 medium yellow onion, diced | 2 teaspoons paprika |
| 1 red bell pepper, seeded and diced | 1½ teaspoons ground cumin |
| 1 large stalk celery, chopped | ½ teaspoon white pepper |
| 2 large cloves garlic, minced | ½ teaspoon salt |
| 1 or 2 red Fresno or jalapeño peppers, | 1 cup dairy milk or soy milk |
| seeded and minced | 2 tablespoons chopped fresh cilantro |

IN A LARGE saucepan, heat the oil. Add the onion, bell pepper, celery, garlic, and chili pepper and cook, stirring, for 5 minutes over medium heat. Add 4 cups water, the sweet potatoes, paprika, cumin, white pepper, and salt and bring to a simmer. Cook over medium-low heat until the potatoes are tender, about 20 minutes, stirring occasionally.

Transfer the soup to a blender or food processor fitted with a steel blade and puree until smooth, about 5 seconds. Return the soup to the pan and stir in the milk and cilantro. Bring the soup to a gentle simmer over medium-low heat.

Ladle the bisque into bowls and serve at once.

YIELD: 6 SERVINGS

### Some Like It Hotter

ADD 1 MORE CHILI PEPPER TO THE SOUP OR USE CAYENNE PEPPER INSTEAD OF WHITE PEPPER.

# Red Fresno Butternut Bisque

THE HEAT OF the red Fresno chili pepper adds a spark to this silky butternut squash soup. Red Fresnos are assertive without being aggressive.

1 tablespoon canola oil

1 medium yellow onion, diced

1 red bell pepper, seeded and
  diced

2 stalks celery, chopped

1 large carrot, diced

4 cloves garlic, minced

2 red Fresno or red jalapeño peppers,
  seeded and minced

2½ cups peeled, coarsely chopped
  butternut squash

2 teaspoons paprika

1 teaspoon ground cumin

1 teaspoon ground coriander

½ teaspoon salt

½ teaspoon cayenne pepper

2 tablespoons chopped fresh cilantro
  (optional)

IN A LARGE saucepan, heat the oil. Add the onion, bell pepper, celery, carrot, garlic, and chilies and cook, stirring, for 5 to 6 minutes over medium heat. Add 2 cups water, the squash, paprika, cumin, coriander, salt, and cayenne pepper and bring to a simmer. Cook over medium-low heat until the squash is tender, about 20 minutes, stirring occasionally.

Transfer the soup to a blender or food processor fitted with a steel blade and puree until smooth, about 5 seconds. Return the soup to the pan and stir in the optional cilantro. Ladle the bisque into bowls and serve at once.

YIELD: 6 SERVINGS

## Spice Advice

ADD A DOLLOP OF PLAIN YOGURT TO THE BOWLS JUST BEFORE SERVING.

# Black and White Bean Soup

FOR THIS SNAZZY soup, pureed white beans are swirled into the black bean soup at the finish.

| | |
|---|---|
| 2 tablespoons canola oil | 1 tablespoon chili powder |
| 2 medium yellow onions, diced | 2 teaspoons dried oregano |
| 1 green bell pepper, seeded and diced | 1½ teaspoons ground cumin |
| 2 stalks celery, chopped | ½ teaspoon salt |
| 2 cans (15 ounces each) black beans | 4 cloves garlic, minced |
| 1 cup canned crushed tomatoes | 1 can (15 ounces) white kidney beans |
| 1 cup water or vegetable broth | ¼ cup dry white wine |
| 2 tablespoons chopped pickled jalapeños | 2 tablespoons chopped parsley |
| | ½ cup shredded Monterey Jack cheese |

IN A LARGE saucepan, heat 1 tablespoon of the oil. Add half the onions, the bell pepper, and celery and cook, stirring, for 5 minutes over medium heat. Add the black beans, crushed tomatoes, water, pickled jalapeños, chili powder, oregano, cumin, and salt and bring to a simmer. Cook for 15 minutes over medium-low heat, stirring occasionally. Transfer to a blender or food processor fitted with a steel blade and puree until smooth, about 5 seconds. Return the soup to the pan.

Meanwhile, in a medium saucepan, heat the remaining 1 tablespoon oil. Add the remaining onion and the garlic and cook, stirring, for 4 minutes over medium heat. Add the white beans, wine, and parsley and bring to a simmer. Cook, stirring, for 7 to 10 minutes over medium heat. Transfer to a blender or food processor fitted with a steel blade and puree until smooth, about 5 seconds. Return the white bean puree to the pan and stir in the cheese.

To serve, ladle the black bean soup into bowls (up to three-quarters full). Swirl a few tablespoons of the white bean puree into the soup. Serve at once.

YIELD: 4 SERVINGS

# New Mexico Chili Vichyssoise

NEW MEXICO CHILIES transform this potato bisque into a savory bowl of iridescent flavors.

| | |
|---|---|
| 3 or 4 dried New Mexico chilies, seeded | 2½ cups peeled, diced potatoes |
| 1 cup simmering water | 2 carrots, diced |
| 1 tablespoon canola oil | 1 teaspoon paprika |
| 1 red bell pepper, seeded and diced | 1 teaspoon ground cumin |
| 1 medium yellow onion, diced | ½ teaspoon white pepper |
| 2 stalks celery, diced | ½ teaspoon salt |
| 3 or 4 cloves garlic, minced | 1 cup milk or light cream |

HEAT AN UNGREASED skillet and add the chilies. Cook over medium heat until lightly toasted, about 2 minutes. Shake the pan and turn the chilies as they cook. Remove from the heat and cover the chilies with the simmering water. Soak for 15 to 20 minutes. Place a lid or plate over the chilies to keep them from floating. Drain the liquid (save some of the liquid if you plan to add it to the soup; see "Some Like It Hotter") and coarsely chop the chilies.

In a large saucepan, heat the oil. Add the bell pepper, onion, celery, and garlic and cook, stirring, for 6 minutes over medium-high heat. Add 4 cups water, the potatoes, carrots, paprika, cumin, white pepper, and salt and bring to a simmer. Add the chilies and cook over medium-low heat until the potatoes are tender, 20 to 25 minutes, stirring occasionally.

Transfer the soup to a food processor fitted with a steel blade or to a blender and process until smooth, about 5 seconds. Return the pureed soup to the pan and stir in the milk. Bring to a gentle simmer over low heat. Ladle the vichyssoise into bowls and serve hot.

YIELD: 6 SERVINGS

### Some Like It Hotter

ADD ½ CUP OF THE CHILIES
SOAKING LIQUID TO THE SOUP
AS IT SIMMERS. ADDING A
SEEDED AND MINCED RED
FRESNO OR RED JALAPEÑO IS
ALSO A SPICE OPTION.

# Poblano Chicken Posole

ROASTED POBLANO CHILIES give this hearty Southwestern chili-stew a smoky flavor.

2 or 3 large poblano chilies, cored and
    seeded

1 tablespoon canola oil

1 medium yellow onion, diced

2 stalks celery, diced

3 or 4 cloves garlic, minced

¾ pound boneless chicken thighs, diced

1 can (28 ounces) plum tomatoes

1 can (14 ounces) crushed tomatoes

1 can (14 ounces) corn hominy,
    drained

1 tablespoon dried oregano

1½ teaspoons ground cumin

1½ teaspoons chili powder

½ teaspoon black pepper

½ teaspoon salt

To ROAST THE poblano chilies, place them over a hot grill or beneath a preheated broiler for 4 to 5 minutes on each side until the skin is charred. Remove from the heat and let cool for a few minutes. Using a butter knife, peel off the charred skin. Chop the flesh.

In a large saucepan, heat the oil. Add the onion, celery, and garlic and cook, stirring, for 5 minutes over medium-high heat. Stir in the chicken and cook, stirring, for 4 minutes more. Stir in the poblanos, plum tomatoes, crushed tomatoes, hominy, oregano, cumin, chili powder, black pepper, and salt and bring to a simmer. Cook for about 20 minutes over medium-low heat, stirring occasionally. Remove from the heat and let stand for 5 to 10 minutes before serving.

Ladle the posole into bowls and serve at once with plenty of warm flour tortillas.

YIELD: 6 SERVINGS

🍴 *Shopping Tip*

LOOK FOR HOMINY IN THE CANNED GOODS AISLE OF WELL-STOCKED SUPERMARKETS.

# New Mexico Chili-Stew

NEW MEXICO CHILIES are to the Southwest kitchen what garlic is to the Italian kitchen. Both fresh and dried chilies are used to invigorate myriad soups, stews, and sauces.

This is an especially good stew to prepare when you are expecting vegetarian guests.

| | |
|---|---|
| 2 or 3 dried New Mexico chilies, seeded | 4 cups water or vegetable broth |
| 1 cup simmering water | 1 large potato, peeled and diced |
| 2 tablespoons canola oil | 1½ cups corn kernels, fresh or frozen |
| 1 large yellow onion, diced | 1 tablespoon dried parsley |
| 1 red bell pepper, seeded and diced | 2 teaspoons dried oregano |
| 1 medium zucchini, diced | 1½ teaspoons ground cumin |
| 2 large cloves garlic, minced | 1 teaspoon salt |
| 1 can (14 ounces) stewed tomatoes | ¼ cup tomato paste |

HEAT AN UNGREASED skillet and add the chilies. Cook over medium heat until lightly toasted, about 2 minutes. Shake the pan and occasionally turn the chilies. Remove from the heat and cover the chilies with the simmering water. Soak for 15 to 20 minutes. Place a lid or plate over the chilies to keep them from floating. Put the chilies and ½ cup of the soaking liquid in a blender or food processor fitted with a steel blade and process until pureed, about 5 seconds. Scrape the chilies into a small bowl.

In a large saucepan, heat the oil. Add the onion, bell pepper, zucchini, and garlic and cook, stirring, for 6 minutes over medium heat. Stir in the pureed chilies, stewed tomatoes, water, potato, corn, parsley, oregano, cumin, and salt and bring to a simmer. Cook over medium-low heat until the potatoes are tender, about 20 minutes, stirring occasionally. Stir in the tomato paste and cook for 5 minutes more.

Let the stew stand for 5 to 10 minutes before serving. Ladle into bowls and serve at once.

YIELD: 8 SERVINGS

# Ancho White Bean Chili

ANCHO CHILIES ADD a toasty flavor to this hearty vegetable and bean chili.

2 or 3 ancho or dried New Mexico
    chilies, seeded

1 cup simmering water

1 tablespoon canola oil

1 large yellow onion, diced

1 yellow or red bell pepper, seeded
    and diced

1 medium zucchini, diced

1 large carrot, diced

2 large cloves garlic, minced

1 can (28 ounces) plum tomatoes

1 can (15 ounces) corn kernels, drained

1 can (15 ounces) white kidney
    beans, drained

1 tablespoon dried parsley

1 tablespoon dried oregano

2 teaspoons ground cumin

2 to 3 teaspoons chili powder

½ teaspoon black pepper

½ teaspoon salt

2 tablespoons chopped fresh cilantro
    (optional)

HEAT AN UNGREASED skillet and add the chilies. Cook over medium heat until lightly toasted, about 2 minutes. Shake the pan and turn the chilies as they cook. Remove from the heat and cover the chilies with the simmering water. Soak for 15 to 20 minutes. Cover the chilies with a lid or plate to keep them from floating. Put the chilies and ½ cup of the soaking liquid in a blender or food processor fitted with a steel blade and process until pureed, about 5 seconds. Scrape the chilies into a small bowl.

In a large saucepan, heat the oil. Add the onion, bell pepper, zucchini, carrot, and garlic and cook, stirring, for 6 minutes over medium heat. Stir in the plum tomatoes, corn, beans, parsley, oregano, cumin, chili powder, black pepper, salt, and pureed chilies and bring to a simmer. Cook for 15 minutes over medium-low heat, stirring occasionally.

Remove the pan from the heat and stir in the optional cilantro. Let stand for 5 to 10 minutes before serving.

YIELD: 6 SERVINGS

### Spice Advice

TOP THE BOWLS WITH
SHREDDED MONTEREY JACK OR
PROVOLONE CHEESE.

# Cayenne Black Bean Posole

FRESH AND DRIED cayenne peppers provide a combustible jolt to this tomato-based stew of beans and hominy.

1 tablespoon canola oil

1 medium yellow onion, diced

1 red bell pepper, seeded and diced

2 stalks celery, chopped

4 cloves garlic, minced

2 fresh cayenne chili peppers, seeded
    and minced

1 can (28 ounces) tomato puree

1 can (15 ounces) black beans,
    drained

1 can (14 ounces) corn hominy,
    drained

1 tablespoon dried oregano

1 tablespoon chili powder

½ teaspoon cayenne pepper

½ teaspoon salt

IN A LARGE saucepan, heat the oil. Add the onion, bell pepper, celery, garlic, and cayenne chili peppers and cook, stirring, for 5 to 7 minutes over medium-high heat. Stir in the tomato puree, beans, hominy, ½ cup water, oregano, chili powder, cayenne pepper, and salt and bring to a simmer. Cook for 15 minutes over medium-low heat, stirring occasionally. Remove from the heat and let stand for 5 minutes before serving.

Ladle the posole into bowls. Serve with corn bread or flour tortillas.

YIELD: 4 SERVINGS

### Shopping Tip

LOOK FOR HOMINY IN THE CANNED GOODS AISLE OF WELL-STOCKED SUPERMARKETS.

# CHAPTER THREE

# Bowls in Paradise

## A TASTE OF THE CARIBBEAN

THE CARIBBEAN IS known for pristine beaches, turquoise waters, swaying palm trees . . . and tempting bowls of fire and spice. From Bahamian Conch Chowder, Jamaican Chicken Curry, and St. Lucian Squash Bisque to Seafood Callaloo Pepperpot and Fiery Chicken Congo, this chapter offers an enticing array of high-spirited soups, pepperpots, curries, and bisques. To connoisseurs of spicy food, Caribbean cooking is paradise found.

In my pursuit of culinary adventures, I have traveled often to the Caribbean. I have tasted and traipsed my way through a bounty of sizzling cauldrons, indulged in the scorching island hot sauces, and cooled my palate with soothing piña coladas. Italy loves its garlic and basil; Asia treasures its ginger and soy sauce. The Caribbean relishes its pungent peppers.

Easily the most famous Caribbean pepper is the **Scotch bonnet pepper,** a curvaceous, lantern-shaped pod with a wicked, turbocharged heat and floral nuance. Also called country pepper or Bahama mama, the Scotch bonnet comes in rainbow green, red, orange, and yellow and has an ornamental, primal appearance (no two chilies seem to look alike). Scotch

37

bonnets are considered to be the hottest chilies in the world and are interchangeable with habaneros, their close cousins.

Scotch bonnet look-alikes are enjoyed throughout the Caribbean. On a trip to Barbados, I discovered **bonney peppers,** fire-engine-red and bright-yellow pods with sleek curvatures. Bonney peppers inspire a pantheon of Bajan yellow hot sauces. On St. Lucia, a lush island with a Creole heritage, are explosive red, green, and yellow chilies called **pimient ma jacks.** Trinidad and Tobago, the West Indian capital of curry, is the home of the **Congo pepper,** a flammable chili with a striking resemblance to the Scotch bonnet. Congo peppers have inspired legions of island hot sauces. In the Bahamas, colorful **goat peppers** jazz up conch salads, chowders, curries, and stews.

Not all Caribbean peppers are blazing hot. **Rocatillos,** also called aji dulces, are neon-colored pods that look like miniature pattypan squash. The peppers, which have a tangy, citrusy flavor, are a key ingredient in sofrito, an aromatic mirepoix-style base used to enhance a variety of soups, sancochos (stews), and asopao, a soupy chicken-and-rice dish similar to paella. The **seasoning pepper** from Grenada is another pod with citrusy-sweet heat.

Though the Caribbean is not the birthplace of hot peppers (experts place the initial hot zone somewhere near the Bolivian-Brazilian borders), chilies have been cultivated on the islands for centuries. A well-known legend holds that when Christopher Columbus sailed for the East Indies in search of peppercorns, he instead found the native Arawaks and Caribs lacing their food with red hot chili peppers. Thinking the spicy pods were related to black peppercorns, Columbus mistakenly called them "peppers." Botanically speaking, chilies are not related to the peppercorn family, but the misnomer stuck.

While it would be incorrect to credit Columbus with "discovering" chili peppers—they had been cultivated long before he and his travelers arrived in the New World—he did open up the gates to Europe and Asia. Seafarers transported chili pepper plants and seeds to every corner of the globe, and soon the cultures of India, Southeast Asia, Africa, and Europe were introduced to the glories of hot peppers. It is safe to say that many of the world's chili peppers—Hungarian paprikas, Thai bird peppers, Indian cayennes, and so on—can be traced to a Caribbean port of call hundreds of years ago.

The Caribbean pantry also includes large West Indian pumpkins called calabaza, red and black beans, rice, plantains, tubers such as dasheen and yellow yam, mangoes, papayas, and coconuts. Thyme and parsley grow rampant, while native allspice, nutmeg, and cloves add sweet nuances to the pot. Curry, an adopted spice blend from India, has also become a signature flavor in island kitchens.

# Grenadian Pumpkin Bisque

BOWLS IN GRENADA are flavored with seasoning peppers, small bright chilies with a fleeting but enchanted heat. Although seasoning peppers are hard to find in America, combining a sweet red pepper with a small serrano is a close substitute.

1 tablespoon canola oil

1 medium yellow onion, diced

1 red bell pepper, diced

1 large tomato, diced

3 or 4 cloves garlic, minced

1 serrano pepper, seeded and minced

4 cups peeled, diced West Indian pumpkin or butternut squash

1 tablespoon curry powder

1½ teaspoons ground cumin

1 teaspoon salt

½ teaspoon black pepper

¼ teaspoon turmeric

4 scallions, chopped

IN A LARGE saucepan, heat the oil. Add the onion, bell pepper, tomato, garlic, and serrano and cook, stirring, for 6 to 7 minutes over medium heat. Stir in the pumpkin, curry powder, cumin, salt, black pepper, and turmeric and cook, stirring, for 2 minutes more. Add 5 cups water and bring to a simmer. Cook over medium-low heat until the squash is tender, 20 to 25 minutes, stirring occasionally.

Transfer the soup to a food processor fitted with a steel blade or to a blender and process until smooth, about 5 seconds.

Ladle the bisque into bowls and shower the scallions over the top. Serve at once.

YIELD: 6 SERVINGS

### ♈ Shopping Tip

WEST INDIAN PUMPKIN, ALSO CALLED CALABAZA, IS AVAILABLE IN CARIBBEAN AND LATIN AMERICAN MARKETS AND OCCASIONALLY AT WELL-STOCKED SUPERMARKETS. THE HUGE GOURDS HAVE A BRIGHT ORANGE FLESH AND A FLAVOR SIMILAR TO THAT OF A SWEET POTATO. BUTTERNUT OR HUBBARD SQUASH MAY BE SUBSTITUTED.

# Seafood Callaloo Pepperpot

THE FABLED SCOTCH bonnet peppers energize this spicy coconut broth of mixed shellfish, squash, and callaloo greens. Callaloo is a cross between spinach and collard greens.

1 tablespoon canola oil

1 large yellow onion, diced

1 red bell pepper, seeded and diced

2 or 3 cloves garlic, minced

1 Scotch bonnet pepper, seeded and
  minced

6 cups fish stock or chicken broth

½ pound callaloo or spinach leaves,
  coarsely chopped

2 cups diced West Indian pumpkin or
  winter squash

¼ cup dark rum

1½ teaspoons dried thyme

1 teaspoon salt

½ teaspoon black pepper

1½ cups canned coconut milk

½ pound precooked lump crab meat,
  cartilage removed (thawed, if
  frozen)

½ pound medium shrimp, peeled and
  deveined

¼ cup chopped fresh parsley

IN A LARGE saucepan, heat the oil. Add the onion, bell pepper, garlic, and Scotch bonnet pepper and cook, stirring, for 5 minutes over medium heat. Add the stock, callaloo, pumpkin, rum, thyme, salt, and black pepper and bring to a simmer. Cook for 15 minutes over medium heat, stirring occasionally. Stir in the coconut milk, crab meat, shrimp, and parsley and return to a simmer. Cook for 15 minutes over medium-low heat, stirring occasionally. To thicken, mash the pumpkin against the side of the pan with the back of a spoon.

Ladle the pepperpot into bowls and serve at once. Accompany the dish with plenty of bread.

YIELD: 8 SERVINGS

### ♨ Shopping Tip

CALLALOO IS HARD TO FIND IN THE UNITED STATES, BUT SPINACH CAN BE SUBSTITUTED. WEST INDIAN PUMPKIN, ALSO CALLED CALABAZA, IS AVAILABLE IN CARIBBEAN AND LATIN AMERICAN MARKETS AND OCCASIONALLY AT WELL-STOCKED SUPERMARKETS. BUTTERNUT OR HUBBARD SQUASH MAY BE SUBSTITUTED.

# Jamaican Red Pea Soup

RED KIDNEY BEANS, known as red peas in Jamaica, are a favorite soup staple. This version is spiced with Scotch bonnet peppers, coconut, thyme, and allspice (which is known as Jamaican pimiento).

| | |
|---|---|
| 1 cup red kidney beans, soaked overnight and drained | 4 whole scallions, halved |
| 1 tablespoon canola oil | 1 large sweet potato, diced |
| 1 large yellow onion, diced | 1½ teaspoons dried thyme |
| 1 large green bell pepper, seeded and diced | ½ teaspoon black pepper |
| 4 cloves garlic, minced | ¼ teaspoon ground allspice |
| 1 Scotch bonnet pepper, seeded and minced | 1 cup canned crushed tomatoes |
| | 1 cup canned coconut milk |
| | 2 tablespoons chopped fresh parsley |
| | 1 teaspoon salt |

IN A LARGE saucepan, combine the beans and 7 cups water and bring to a simmer. Cook over medium-low heat until the beans are tender, 1 to 1½ hours, stirring occasionally.

Meanwhile, in another large saucepan, heat the oil. Add the onion, bell pepper, garlic, and Scotch bonnet pepper and cook, stirring, for 5 to 6 minutes over medium heat. Add the cooked beans, cooking liquid, scallions, sweet potato, thyme, black pepper, and allspice. Bring to a simmer and cook for 20 minutes over medium-low heat, stirring occasionally.

Stir in the crushed tomatoes, coconut milk, parsley, and salt and return to a gentle simmer. Cook, stirring, for 5 minutes more over low heat. To thicken, ladle one-third of the soup into a food processor fitted with a steel blade or into a blender and process until smooth, about 5 seconds. Return the pureed soup to the pan and stir.

Ladle the soup into bowls and serve at once with plenty of good crusty bread.

YIELD: 6 SERVINGS

**Spice Advice**

RED PEA SOUP CAN ALSO INCLUDE CARROTS, POTATOES, WEST INDIAN PUMPKIN, SPINACH, OR WHATEVER IS IN SEASON.

# Spicy Caribbean Greens Bisque

THE FAVORITE LEAFY green in the Caribbean is callaloo, a cross between spinach and collard greens. I have tasted variations of callaloo soup on Grenada, St. Lucia, and St. Martin, and all have left my palate wanting more.

| | |
|---|---|
| 1 tablespoon olive oil | 2 cups peeled, diced potatoes |
| 1 medium yellow onion, diced | ½ teaspoon dried thyme |
| 4 cloves garlic, minced | ½ teaspoon white pepper |
| ½ Scotch bonnet pepper, seeded and minced | ½ teaspoon salt |
| | ¼ teaspoon ground nutmeg |
| 8 cups coarsely chopped spinach or callaloo greens | ¼ cup canned coconut milk (optional) |
| | ¼ cup chopped fresh parsley |

IN A LARGE saucepan, heat the oil. Add the onion, garlic, and Scotch bonnet pepper and cook, stirring, for 4 minutes over medium heat. Add the spinach and cook, stirring, until wilted, about 2 minutes. Add 4 cups water, the potatoes, thyme, white pepper, salt, and nutmeg and bring to a simmer. Cook until the potatoes are tender, about 20 minutes, stirring occasionally. Stir in the optional coconut milk and the parsley.

Transfer the soup to a blender or food processor fitted with a steel blade and process until smooth, about 10 seconds. Ladle the bisque into bowls and serve at once.

YIELD: 4 SERVINGS

### Shopping Tip

CALLALOO IS HARD TO FIND, BUT SPINACH MAKES AN ACCEPTABLE SUBSTITUTE.

# Vegetable Island Curry

---

THE CARIBBEAN IS a melting pot of cultures and cuisines. India's contribution is the prevalence of aromatic curry dishes that appear on island tables.

1½ tablespoons canola oil

1 medium yellow onion, diced

8 mushrooms, sliced

2 cups diced eggplant

2 medium tomatoes, diced

4 cloves garlic, minced

1 Scotch bonnet pepper, seeded and
    minced

1 tablespoon curry powder

1 teaspoon ground cumin

½ teaspoon turmeric

½ teaspoon salt

2 cups diced potatoes or yellow
    yams

1 cup cooked or canned (drained)
    chick-peas or red kidney beans

3 or 4 cups cooked basmati or long-
    grain white rice

IN A LARGE saucepan, heat the oil. Add the onion, mushrooms, and eggplant and cook, stirring, for 5 minutes over medium heat. Add the tomatoes, garlic, and Scotch bonnet pepper and cook, stirring, for 5 to 7 minutes more. Stir in the curry powder, cumin, turmeric, and salt and cook for 1 minute more.

Add the potatoes and 1½ cups water and bring to a simmer. Cook for 20 minutes over medium heat, stirring occasionally. Stir in the chick-peas and cook, stirring, until the potatoes are tender, about 10 minutes more. Let stand for 5 minutes.

Spoon the rice into bowls and ladle the vegetables over the top.

YIELD: 4 SERVINGS

# Bahamian Conch Chowder

MENTION THE BAHAMAS to anyone who has been there, and conch will surely come to mind. Conch (pronounced "konk"), a chewy kind of shellfish, is on almost every menu from top to bottom. Conch chowder is one of my favorites.

| | |
|---|---|
| 1 tablespoon canola oil | ½ teaspoon black pepper |
| 1 medium yellow onion, diced | 4 cups water or fish stock |
| 1 red bell pepper, seeded and minced | ¾ pound conch meat, chopped |
| 3 or 4 cloves garlic, minced | 1 large potato, diced |
| 1 small Scotch bonnet or habanero pepper, seeded and minced | 1 cup light cream |
| | ½ cup tomato paste |
| 1½ tablespoons curry powder | 2 tablespoons butter |
| 1 teaspoon dried thyme | 2 tablespoons all-purpose |
| 1 teaspoon salt | flour |

IN A LARGE saucepan, heat the oil. Add the onion, bell pepper, garlic, and Scotch bonnet pepper and cook, stirring, for 5 minutes over medium heat. Add curry powder, thyme, salt, and black pepper and cook, stirring, for 1 minute more. Add the water, conch meat, and potato and bring to a simmer. Cook over medium heat until the potatoes are tender, about 20 minutes, stirring occasionally. Reduce the heat to low and stir in the cream and tomato paste. Return to a gentle simmer.

Meanwhile, make the roux: Melt the butter in a skillet over medium heat. Gradually stir in the flour, forming a paste. Cook, stirring, over low heat for 3 to 4 minutes.

Whisk the roux into the simmering chowder and cook, stirring, for 3 minutes more.

Ladle the chowder into bowls and serve at once.

YIELD: 6 SERVINGS

🍴 *Shopping Tip*

CONCH MEAT IS AVAILABLE ON A SEASONAL BASIS AT FISH MARKETS AND AT WELL-STOCKED SUPERMARKETS. SQUID OR CLAM STRIPS CAN BE SUBSTITUTED FOR A SIMILAR (AND STILL TASTY) CHOWDER.

# Ocean Pepperpot

IT SEEMS EVERY island has a bustling seaport where fish boats bring in the day's catch from the ocean. The bounty of fresh seafood inspires myriad soups, stews, and pepperpots.

Although pepperpots vary from island to island, you will always find a thirst-quenching island beverage at the table. Serve this with a piña colada, rum punch, or an island beer, such as Red Stripe.

| | |
|---|---|
| 1 tablespoon canola oil | 1 teaspoon dried thyme |
| 1 medium yellow onion, diced | ½ teaspoon black pepper |
| 1 green bell pepper, seeded and diced | ½ teaspoon salt |
| 2 stalks celery, chopped | ½ pound scallops or medium shrimp, |
| 4 cloves garlic, minced |     peeled and deveined |
| 1 small Scotch bonnet pepper or 2 ser- | ½ pound boneless white fish fillets |
|     rano peppers, seeded and minced |     (such as cod or sole), cubed |
| 3 cups clam juice or fish stock | 1 can (11 ounces) corn kernels, |
| 2 cups diced potatoes |     drained |
| 1 can (14 ounces) stewed tomatoes | 1 cup light cream or milk |
| 2 teaspoons dried oregano | ½ cup tomato paste |

IN A LARGE saucepan, heat the oil. Add the onion, bell pepper, celery, garlic, and chili pepper and cook, stirring, for 6 minutes over medium-high heat. Add the clam juice, 2 cups water, the potatoes, stewed tomatoes, oregano, thyme, black pepper, and salt and bring to a simmer. Cook for 10 minutes over medium heat, stirring occasionally.

Stir in the scallops and fish fillets and return to a simmer. Cook for 15 to 20 minutes over medium heat, stirring occasionally. Stir in the corn, cream, and tomato paste and cook for 5 to 10 minutes over low heat.

Ladle the pepperpot into large bowls and serve at once with warm French bread.

YIELD: 8 SERVINGS

### ♈ Shopping Tip

CLAM JUICE IS
AVAILABLE IN MOST
WELL-STOCKED
SUPERMARKETS.

# St. Lucian Squash Bisque

ST. LUCIA IS home to a variety of vivacious red, green, and yellow chilies known as pimient ma jacks. Similar to Scotch bonnet peppers, the chilies are used in soups, stews, and legions of bottled hot sauces.

For a more flavorful bisque, try using a curry powder imported from India or the Caribbean, which will be stronger than a domestic brand.

*1 tablespoon canola oil*

*1 large yellow onion, diced*

*2 stalks celery, diced*

*4 cloves garlic, minced*

*1 tablespoon minced ginger*
   *root*

*1 Scotch bonnet or habanero*
   *pepper, seeded and minced*

*2 large tomatoes, diced*

*1 tablespoon curry powder*

*1 teaspoon ground cumin*

*1 teaspoon ground coriander*

*1 teaspoon salt*

*4 cups peeled, diced West Indian*
   *pumpkin or butternut squash*

*1 cup milk or light cream*

IN A LARGE saucepan, heat the oil. Add the onion, celery, garlic, ginger, and chili pepper. Cook, stirring, for about 5 minutes over medium heat. Add the tomatoes, curry powder, cumin, coriander, and salt and cook, stirring, for 3 to 4 minutes more. Add the pumpkin and 4½ cups water and bring to a simmer. Cook for 25 to 30 minutes over medium-low heat, stirring occasionally. Stir in the milk and return to a gentle simmer.

Transfer the soup to a food processor fitted with a steel blade or to a blender and process until smooth, about 10 seconds.

Ladle the bisque into bowls and serve at once with plenty of warm crusty bread.

YIELD: 6 SERVINGS

### ℐℐℐ Shopping Tip

WEST INDIAN PUMPKIN, ALSO
CALLED CALABAZA, IS AVAILABLE
IN CARIBBEAN AND LATIN
AMERICAN MARKETS AND
OCCASIONALLY AT WELL-
STOCKED SUPERMARKETS.

# Haitian Hot Pot

HAITIAN CUISINE IS a melting pot of African, Creole, French, and native island cultures. The spicy soups and stews include squash, potatoes, turnips, beans, and, of course, tropical chili peppers.

1 tablespoon canola oil

1 medium yellow onion, diced

1 large green or red bell pepper, seeded and diced

1 stalk celery, diced

3 or 4 cloves garlic, minced

1 Scotch bonnet or habanero pepper, seeded and minced

2 cups diced butternut squash or West Indian pumpkin

2 cups coarsely chopped potatoes

1 medium turnip, peeled and diced

1 tablespoon dried parsley

1 teaspoon dried thyme

1 teaspoon salt

½ teaspoon turmeric

1 can (15 ounces) red kidney beans, drained

IN A LARGE saucepan, heat the oil. Add the onion, bell pepper, celery, garlic, and chili pepper and cook, stirring, for 5 to 6 minutes over medium-high heat. Add 8 cups water, the squash, potatoes, turnip, parsley, thyme, salt, and turmeric and bring to a simmer. Cook for 40 to 45 minutes over medium-low heat, stirring occasionally. Stir in the beans and cook for about 5 minutes more. To thicken, mash the squash and potatoes against the side of the pan with the back of a spoon.

Ladle the stew into bowls and serveat once. Accompany with warm crusty bread.

YIELD: 8 SERVINGS

🍴 *Shopping Tip*

WEST INDIAN PUMPKIN, ALSO CALLED CALABAZA, IS AVAILABLE IN CARIBBEAN AND LATIN AMERICAN MARKETS AND OCCASIONALLY AT WELL-STOCKED SUPERMARKETS.

# Jamaican Chicken Curry

THE NOTORIOUS SCOTCH bonnet peppers turn up the heat in this savory bowl of curried chicken and rice. Offering Jamaican Red Stripe beer at the table might not be such a bad idea!

For a more authentic flavor, use a curry powder with an Indian or Caribbean brand name. Ethnic curry powders seem to have more "bite" to them than domestic brands do.

1 tablespoon canola oil

1 large yellow onion, diced

3 or 4 cloves garlic, minced

1 or 2 Scotch bonnet peppers, seeded and minced

2 medium tomatoes, diced

3 to 4 teaspoons curry powder

1 teaspoon ground cumin

½ teaspoon black pepper

½ teaspoon salt

¼ teaspoon turmeric

1 pound boneless chicken thighs or breasts, diced

2 cups water or chicken broth

2 carrots, diced

2 cups diced potatoes

1 can (15 ounces) chick-peas, drained

3 to 4 cups cooked jasmine, basmati, or long-grain white rice

IN A LARGE saucepan, heat the oil. Add the onion, garlic, and Scotch bonnet pepper and cook, stirring, for about 4 minutes over medium-high heat. Add the tomatoes, curry powder, cumin, black pepper, salt, and turmeric and cook, stirring, for 3 minutes more. Stir in the chicken and cook, stirring, for 4 minutes more. Add the water, carrots, potatoes, and chick-peas and bring to a simmer. Cook for 20 to 25 minutes over medium heat until the chicken is fully cooked, stirring occasionally.

Spoon the rice into bowls and ladle the curried chicken over the top. Serve at once.

YIELD: 4 SERVINGS

**℮ Some Like It Hotter**

OFFER A BOTTLE OF CARIBBEAN

HOT SAUCE AT THE TABLE.

# Trinidadian Shrimp Pilau

THE FLAVORS OF this pilaf-style dish are a harmonic blend of garlic, ginger, chili peppers, curry, and nutty coconut.

For a stronger curry flavor, try a curry powder imported from India or the Caribbean.

2 tablespoons canola oil

1 medium yellow onion, diced

1 red bell pepper, seeded and diced

8 ounces mushrooms, sliced

2 large cloves garlic, minced

1 tablespoon minced ginger root

2 serrano peppers or ½ Scotch bonnet pepper, seeded and minced

1½ cups long-grain white or basmati rice

1 cup canned coconut milk

1 cup canned pigeon peas or red chili beans

1 tablespoon dried parsley

2 to 3 teaspoons curry powder

1 teaspoon dried thyme

1 teaspoon salt

½ teaspoon black pepper

½ teaspoon ground turmeric

¾ to 1 pound medium shrimp, peeled and deveined

4 scallions, chopped

IN A LARGE saucepan, heat the oil. Add the onion, bell pepper, mushrooms, garlic, ginger, and chili pepper and cook, stirring, for 7 to 8 minutes over medium heat. Stir in 2 cups water, the rice, coconut milk, pigeon peas, parsley, curry powder, thyme, salt, black pepper, and turmeric and bring to a simmer. Stir in the shrimp and cover. Cook over medium-low heat until all of the liquid is absorbed, 15 to 20 minutes.

Fluff the grains and shrimp and fold in the scallions. Let stand (covered) for about 5 minutes. Spoon the pilau into bowls and serve while still hot.

YIELD: 4 SERVINGS

🍴 *Shopping Tip*

PIGEON PEAS ARE SMALL, PEA-SHAPED BEANS USUALLY AVAILABLE IN WELL-STOCKED SUPERMARKETS AND LATIN AMERICAN OR CARIBBEAN GROCERY STORES.

🐛 *Some Like It Hotter*

PASS A BOTTLE OF CARIBBEAN HOT SAUCE AT THE TABLE.

# West Indian Beef Sancocho

SANCOCHO IS A hearty Caribe stew of root vegetables, plantains, legumes, and assorted meats. Think of it as an island version of pot-au-feu.

Adding pierced, whole Scotch bonnet peppers is a more subtle way of incorporating the flavor than adding minced peppers. But be careful not to bite into the whole pods!

1 tablespoon canola oil

1 medium yellow onion, diced

1 red bell pepper, seeded and diced

3 or 4 cloves garlic, minced

1 pound top round or sirloin tip, cubed

6 cups water or chicken broth

½ cup lentils

2 cups peeled, diced West Indian pumpkin or butternut squash

1 medium potato, diced

1 greenish-yellow plantain, peeled and thickly sliced

2 whole Scotch bonnet peppers, pierced with a fork

1 tablespoon dried parsley

1 teaspoon dried thyme

½ teaspoon black pepper

½ teaspoon turmeric

1 teaspoon salt

IN A LARGE saucepan, heat the oil. Add the onion, bell pepper, and garlic and cook, stirring, for 4 minutes over medium-high heat. Add the beef and cook, stirring, until browned, about 5 minutes. Add the water and lentils and bring to a simmer. Cook for 10 minutes over medium heat, stirring occasionally. Add the pumpkin, potato, plantain, Scotch bonnet peppers, parsley, thyme, black pepper, and turmeric and cook over medium heat until the lentils and vegetables are tender, 35 to 45 minutes, stirring occasionally. Remove the Scotch bonnet peppers and stir in the salt.

Ladle the stew into bowls and serve at once. If desired, cut the peppers into strips and serve on the side.

YIELD: 6 SERVINGS

### ᵞᵞᵞ Shopping Tip

YOU CAN FIND PLANTAINS AND WEST INDIAN PUMPKIN IN CARIBBEAN AND HISPANIC MARKETS OR AT WELL-STOCKED SUPERMARKETS. OTHER CARIBBEAN ROOT VEGETABLES, SUCH AS DASHEEN, YELLOW YAM, OR TARO, CAN ALSO BE USED.

# Fiery Chicken Congo

CONGO PEPPERS FROM Trinidad lend a searing heat to this sweltering bowl of curried chicken and vegetables. Scotch bonnets or habaneros may also be used.

1 tablespoon canola oil

1 medium yellow onion, diced

1 medium tomato, diced

4 cloves garlic, minced

1 or 2 Congo peppers or other fiery peppers, seeded and minced

1 tablespoon minced ginger root

1 tablespoon curry powder

1 teaspoon ground cumin

½ teaspoon turmeric

½ teaspoon salt

1 pound boneless chicken thighs or breasts, diced

2 carrots, diced

1 large potato, diced

1½ cups chicken broth or water

IN A MEDIUM saucepan, heat the oil. Add the onion, tomato, garlic, chili pepper, and ginger and cook, stirring, for about 5 minutes over medium-high heat. Add the curry powder, cumin, turmeric, and salt and cook, stirring, for 1 minute over medium heat. Add the chicken and cook, stirring, for 5 minutes more.

Add the carrots, potato, and broth and bring to a simmer. Cook for 20 to 25 minutes over medium heat, stirring occasionally, until the vegetables are tender and the chicken is fully cooked. Remove from the heat and let stand for about 5 minutes before serving. Ladle the curried chicken into bowls and serve with rice (or rice and beans) on the side or as a bed.

YIELD: 3 OR 4 SERVINGS

# "Jump Up" Rice and Beans

THIS CARIBBEAN SPECIALTY is a pilaf-style dish in which anything goes. ("Jump up" means it is time to party.)

1 tablespoon canola oil

1 medium yellow onion, diced

2 or 3 cloves garlic, minced

1 Scotch bonnet or habanero pepper, seeded and minced

2 cups peeled, diced West Indian pumpkin or butternut squash

2 teaspoons curry powder

½ teaspoon black pepper

½ teaspoon salt

1 cup canned coconut milk

2 cups long-grain white rice

1 can (15 ounces) red kidney beans, drained

IN A LARGE saucepan, heat the oil over medium heat. Add the onion, garlic, and chili pepper and cook, stirring, for 4 minutes. Add the pumpkin, curry powder, black pepper, and salt and cook for 1 minute more.

Stir in 3 cups water, the coconut milk, rice, and beans and bring to a simmer. Cover and cook over medium-low heat for 15 to 20 minutes. Fluff the rice and let stand (still covered) for 10 minutes before serving.

Spoon the rice mixture into bowls and serve at once.

YIELD: 4 TO 6 SERVINGS

### Shopping Tip

WEST INDIAN PUMPKIN, ALSO CALLED CALABAZA, IS AVAILABLE IN CARIBBEAN AND LATIN AMERICAN MARKETS AND OCCASIONALLY AT WELL-STOCKED SUPERMARKETS. CARROTS, LEAFY GREENS, OR SWEET POTATOES CAN ALSO BE ADDED TO THE POT.

# Jamaican Cook-Up Rice

"COOK-UP RICE" IS a one-pot meal consisting of whatever vegetables happen to be in the kitchen.

1 tablespoon canola oil

1 medium yellow onion, diced

1 green or red bell pepper, seeded and diced

1 small zucchini, diced

8 to 10 mushrooms, sliced

½ to 1 Scotch bonnet pepper, seeded and minced

1 cup canned coconut milk

1½ cups long-grain white rice

2 cups peeled, diced winter squash (such as butternut, red kuri, or West Indian pumpkin) or sweet potato

2 tablespoons dried parsley

1 teaspoon dried thyme

½ teaspoon ground allspice

½ teaspoon salt

2 cups chopped leafy greens (such as kale, chard, or spinach)

IN A LARGE saucepan, heat the oil. Add the onion, bell pepper, zucchini, mushrooms, and Scotch bonnet pepper. Cook, stirring, for 5 to 7 minutes over medium-high heat. Add 2¼ cups water, the coconut milk, rice, squash, parsley, thyme, allspice, and salt and bring to a simmer. Cover and cook for about 20 minutes over low heat.

Fluff the rice and stir in the greens. Let stand for about 10 minutes before serving.

YIELD: 4 TO 6 SERVINGS

# CHAPTER FOUR

# Hot Hits the Spot

## CHILI, GUMBO, AND JAMBALAYA

CHILI, GUMBO, AND jambalaya are as American as apple pie and baseball. Believe it or not, this wasn't always the case. Historically, the Yankee palate has been rooted in a Eurocentric culture moored to bland and mild foods. However, in Texas and Louisiana, a half-continent away from Plymouth Rock, spicy kettles and hot pots simmered in kitchens and over campfires. It may have taken a while (about a hundred years), but Tex-Mex, Cajun, and Creole dishes eventually introduced the rest of the country to the thrills of hot-and-spicy cuisine.

Legend traces the origins of chili to nineteenth-century cowboys. While out on the range, the story goes, cowboys spiced up their campfire stews with a pungent blend of dried spices and hot chili peppers. This chili-stew evolved into chili con carne, a meaty one-pot meal, and aficionados later coined the term "bowl of red." Over the years, chili has attracted a devoted and passionate following. Along came the community cook-offs, recipe contests, fan clubs, and an exhausting collection of cookbooks. It seems almost everyone has a favorite chili recipe written down on a dog-eared piece of paper or in a tattered cookbook.

One of the secrets to developing a masterful and flavorful chili is to use a first-rate chili powder. The aromatic blend of spices should include varying amounts of ground red peppers, cumin, paprika, oregano, and garlic powder (salt should not be listed as a main ingredient). A superior chili powder has a strong, musky scent and a dark, burnt-red hue. It pays to shop around, as some commercial brands are better than others. Resourceful chefs mix up their own chili powder, but the rest of us find a quality brand and doctor it up with cumin, cayenne, paprika, and/or dried herbs.

Today's bowl of chili has dropped its surname "con carne" and now includes a variety of inventive ingredients. A wave of nouveau bowls call for sirloin, black beans, chicken, roasted **poblanos,** shellfish, and myriad legumes and tomatoes. Exotic dried chili peppers have entered the mix as well. Chili recipes often feature **ancho, chipotle, New Mexico, habanero,** and other pungent pods.

It has often been said that while most people in the world eat to live, in Louisiana, people *live to eat.* Gumbo and jambalaya epitomize the down-home, "anything goes" nature of Cajun and Creole cooking. ("Gumbo" comes from the African word for okra; "jambalaya" has roots in the French *jambon* for ham.) Gumbo and jambalaya recipes include everything from shrimp, meat, and chicken to spicy sausages, oysters, pork, and lobster. Bottled hot sauces made from Tabasco and/or cayenne chili peppers often provide a splash of heat. Plenty of rice and red beans are used to soak up the fiery, well-rounded flavors in these dynamic dishes.

Most gumbos and jambalayas rely upon a trio of assertive spices: black pepper, white pepper, and cayenne pepper. When used in unison, this feisty triad leaves a pleasurable, well-balanced zing inside the mouth and on the lips. In addition, fresh and dried herbs such as parsley, oregano, and thyme provide an herbal twist to the plot (and pot). Of course, another trio—green peppers, onions, and celery—is used so often that Louisiana cooks refer to them as the "holy trinity."

From New York Sirloin Chili, Chorizo-Chicken Jambalaya, and Wild Mushroom and Chicken Gumbo to Jay's Mondo Chili and Gonzo Gumbo, this chapter beckons with an innovative and enticing array of bowls of fire. This is Americana at its best.

# Seafood "Dirty" Rice

THIS CAJUN DISH is soupy like risotto, hearty like jambalaya, and spicy like gumbo.

For a tasty variation, use basmati or Wild Pecan rice. These grains have a nutty, popcorn-like aroma and are available in well-stocked supermarkets.

1 tablespoon canola oil

1 medium yellow onion, diced

1 green bell pepper, seeded and diced

1 large stalk celery, diced

4 cloves garlic, minced

1 cup tomato puree

1 cup water or fish stock

1 teaspoon dried oregano

1 teaspoon dried thyme

1 teaspoon salt

½ teaspoon white pepper

½ teaspoon cayenne pepper

½ pound medium shrimp, peeled and deveined

½ pound sea scallops

¼ cup light cream or milk

4 cups cooked long-grain white rice

4 whole scallions, chopped

1 to 2 teaspoons bottled red hot sauce

IN A LARGE saucepan, heat the oil. Add the onion, bell pepper, celery, and garlic and cook, stirring, for 6 minutes over medium-high heat. Stir in the tomato puree, water, oregano, thyme, salt, white pepper, and cayenne pepper and bring to a simmer. Add the shrimp and scallops and cook, stirring, over medium heat until the shellfish are opaque, 10 to 12 minutes. Stir in the cream and return to a gentle simmer. Fold in the cooked rice, scallions, and hot sauce.

Spoon the "dirty" rice into shallow bowls and serve while it is still piping hot.

YIELD: 4 SERVINGS

*Some Like It Hotter*

ADD 1 OR 2 JALAPEÑO PEPPERS (SEEDED AND MINCED) ALONG WITH THE VEGETABLES.

# Sixteen-Bean Tureen

A BOWL OF this hearty chili is the perfect antidote for a cold, wintry day.

1 cup sixteen-bean mixture,
    soaked overnight and drained
1 tablespoon canola oil
1 medium yellow onion, diced
1 green or red bell pepper, seeded and
    diced
2 stalks celery, diced
4 cloves garlic, minced

1 can (28 ounces) crushed tomatoes
1 to 2 tablespoons chopped pickled
    jalapeños
1 tablespoon chili powder
2 teaspoons dried oregano
1½ teaspoons dried basil
½ teaspoon cayenne pepper
½ teaspoon salt

IN A LARGE saucepan, combine the sixteen-bean mixture and 7 cups water and bring to a simmer. Cook for about 1½ hours (uncovered) over medium heat until the beans are tender, stirring occasionally. Drain, reserving ½ cup of the cooking liquid.

In another large saucepan, heat the oil. Add the onion, bell pepper, celery, and garlic and cook, stirring, for 5 minutes over medium heat. Stir in the beans, cooking liquid, crushed tomatoes, pickled jalapeños, chili powder, oregano, basil, cayenne pepper, and salt and bring to a simmer. Cook for 15 to 20 minutes over medium-low heat, stirring occasionally. Remove from the heat and let stand for 5 to 10 minutes before serving.

Ladle the chili into bowls and serve at once with plenty of warm Italian bread.

YIELD: 6 SERVINGS

🍴 *Shopping Tip*

PACKAGES OF SIXTEEN-BEAN MIXTURES ARE SOLD IN THE DRIED BEAN SECTIONS OF WELL-STOCKED SUPERMARKETS. REMEMBER TO SOAK THE BEANS IN PLENTY OF WATER FOR SEVERAL HOURS BEFORE COOKING.

🐛 *Some Like It Hotter*

ADD 2 SERRANO PEPPERS OR 1 FRESH CAYENNE PEPPER (SEEDED AND MINCED) TO THE PAN ALONG WITH THE VEGETABLES.

# Eggplant Ratatouille Chili

RATATOUILLE IS A tame Mediterranean vegetable stew. A few hot chili peppers turn the mild to wild, and the tame goes aflame!

1½ tablespoons canola oil

1 tablespoon dry red wine

1 medium yellow onion, diced

1 red bell pepper, seeded and
    diced

2 cups diced eggplant

12 mushrooms, sliced

4 cloves garlic, minced

2 red Fresno or serrano peppers,
    seeded and minced

1 can (28 ounces) plum tomatoes

1 tablespoon chili powder

1 tablespoon dried parsley

2 teaspoons dried oregano

½ teaspoon black pepper

½ teaspoon salt

IN A LARGE saucepan, heat the oil and wine. Add the onion, bell pepper, eggplant, mushrooms, garlic, and chili peppers and cook, stirring, for 8 to 10 minutes over medium heat. Stir in the plum tomatoes, chili powder, parsley, oregano, black pepper, and salt and cook for 15 minutes over medium-low heat, stirring occasionally. Cut the plum tomatoes into smaller pieces with the edge of a spoon as the stew cooks.

Serve the ratatouille in a large bowl over a bed of rice or pasta.

YIELD: 4 SERVINGS

### Some Like It Hotter

DRIZZLE IN A FEW TEASPOONS
OF TABASCO SAUCE AT
THE LAST MINUTE.

# Black Bean and Corn Chili

BLACK BEANS, CORN, and tomatoes turn this chili into a colorful bowl of spicy goodness.

1 tablespoon canola oil

1 medium yellow onion, diced

1 green bell pepper, seeded and diced

2 stalks celery, diced

3 or 4 cloves garlic, minced

1 large jalapeño pepper, seeded and minced

1 can (28 ounces) plum tomatoes

1 can (15 ounces) black beans, drained

1 can (15 ounces) corn kernels, drained

1½ tablespoons chili powder

1 tablespoon dried oregano

1½ teaspoons ground cumin

½ teaspoon black pepper

½ teaspoon salt

1 to 2 teaspoons bottled red hot sauce

IN A LARGE saucepan, heat the oil. Add the onion, bell pepper, celery, garlic, and jalapeño and cook, stirring, for 6 minutes over medium heat. Stir in the plum tomatoes, beans, corn, chili powder, oregano, cumin, black pepper, salt, and hot sauce and bring to a simmer. Cook over medium-low heat for 15 to 18 minutes, stirring occasionally. While the chili cooks, cut the tomatoes into smaller pieces with the edge of a large spoon. Remove the pan from the heat and let stand for 5 to 10 minutes before serving.

Ladle the chili into bowls and serve with warm crusty bread.

YIELD: 4 SERVINGS

### Spice Advice

OFFER LOWFAT YOGURT OR SHREDDED CHEESE AS A TOPPING.

# Chipotle Chicken Chili

CHIPOTLE PEPPERS GIVE this wholesome kettle of chili a vigorous smoky-hot flavor.

| | |
|---|---|
| 2 or 3 dried or canned chipotle chilies, seeded | 1 can (15 ounces) crushed tomatoes |
| ¾ cup simmering water | 1 can (15 ounces) black beans or red kidney beans, drained |
| 1 tablespoon canola oil | |
| 1 medium yellow onion, diced | 1 can (14 ounces) stewed tomatoes |
| 1 red bell pepper, seeded and diced | 1½ tablespoons chili powder |
| 2 stalks celery, diced | 1 tablespoon dried oregano |
| 4 cloves garlic, minced | 1½ teaspoons ground cumin |
| ¾ pound boneless chicken breasts or thighs, diced | ½ teaspoon black pepper |
| | ½ teaspoon salt |

IN A SMALL bowl, cover the dried chilies with the simmering water. Place a lid or plate over the chilies to keep them from floating and soak for 15 minutes. Transfer the chilies and ⅓ cup soaking liquid to a blender or a food processor fitted with a steel blade and process until smooth, about 5 seconds. Scrape the pureed chilies into a small bowl and set aside. (If using canned chipotles, skip this part. Simply mince the chili peppers and add along with the dried seasonings below.)

In a large saucepan, heat the oil. Add the onion, bell pepper, celery, and garlic and cook, stirring, for 5 minutes over medium heat. Stir in the chicken and cook, stirring, for 5 minutes more. Stir in the crushed tomatoes, beans, stewed tomatoes, chili powder, oregano, cumin, black pepper, salt, and pureed chilies (or minced chilies) and bring to a simmer. Cook for 15 to 20 minutes (uncovered) over medium heat, stirring occasionally.

Remove from the heat and let stand for 5 minutes before serving. Ladle the chili-stew into bowls and serve with warm corn bread.

YIELD: 6 SERVINGS

### ♯♯♯ Shopping Tip

LOOK FOR DRIED OR CANNED CHIPOTLE CHILI PEPPERS IN THE MEXICAN SECTION OF WELL-STOCKED SUPERMARKETS.

### ✗ Spice Advice

OFFER PLAIN YOGURT OR SHREDDED MONTEREY JACK CHEESE AS A TOPPING.

# Habanero Fireworks Chili

WITH HABANERO PEPPERS in the pot, you can be assured that the Electric Light Orchestra will be playing in your mouth.

1 tablespoon canola oil

1 medium yellow onion, diced

1 green bell pepper, seeded and
   diced

2 stalks celery, diced

3 or 4 cloves garlic, minced

1 or 2 habanero or Scotch bonnet
   peppers, seeded and minced

1 can (28 ounces) crushed tomatoes

1 can (14 ounces) stewed tomatoes

1 can (15 ounces) pinto beans, drained

1 can (15 ounces) red kidney beans,
   drained

2 tablespoons chili powder

1 tablespoon dried oregano

2 teaspoons ground cumin

½ teaspoon black pepper

½ teaspoon salt

1 to 3 teaspoons bottled Caribbean
   hot sauce

IN A LARGE saucepan, heat the oil. Add the onion, bell pepper, celery, garlic, and chili pepper and cook, stirring, for 6 to 7 minutes over medium-high heat. Add the crushed tomatoes, stewed tomatoes, pinto beans, kidney beans, chili powder, oregano, cumin, black pepper, salt, and hot sauce and bring to a simmer. Cook for 15 to 20 minutes over medium-low heat, stirring occasionally.

Remove the chili from the heat and let stand for 5 minutes before serving. Ladle into bowls and serve with plenty of bread and cool beverages.

YIELD: 4 SERVINGS

## Spice Advice

OFFER LOWFAT YOGURT OR
SHREDDED CHEESE AS A TOPPING.

# New York Sirloin Chili

TENDER SIRLOIN LENDS a gourmet cachet to this chunky, exuberantly flavored chili.

1½ tablespoons canola oil

1 large yellow onion, diced

2 green or red bell peppers, seeded
  and diced

2 stalks celery, diced

4 cloves garlic, minced

2 jalapeño or serrano peppers, seeded
  and minced

¾ pound top sirloin or strip loin, cubed

1 can (28 ounces) crushed tomatoes

1 can (15 ounces) red kidney beans,
  drained

1 can (14 ounces) stewed tomatoes

1½ to 2 tablespoons chili powder

1 tablespoon dried oregano

2 teaspoons ground cumin

1 teaspoon salt

½ teaspoon black pepper

IN A LARGE saucepan, heat the oil. Add the onion, bell peppers, celery, garlic, and chili peppers and cook, stirring, for 6 minutes over medium heat. Stir in the beef and cook, stirring, for 3 to 4 minutes more. Add the crushed tomatoes, beans, stewed tomatoes, chili powder, oregano, cumin, salt, and black pepper and bring to a simmer. Cook for 20 to 25 minutes over medium-low heat, stirring occasionally.

Remove the chili from the heat and let stand for 5 minutes before serving. Ladle the chili into bowls and serve with warm corn bread.

YIELD: 6 SERVINGS

## Spice Advice

OFFER A TOPPING, SUCH AS SHREDDED CHEDDAR OR PROVOLONE CHEESE OR CHOPPED SCALLIONS.

# Jay's Mondo Chili

HERE IS A fun, high-spirited bowl that will please any gourmand of hot-and-spicy cuisine.

Serve the chili with a variety of toppings, such as shredded cheese, guacamole, chopped scallions, or chopped red onions.

1 tablespoon canola oil

1 large yellow onion, diced

1 green bell pepper, seeded and diced

1 red bell pepper, seeded and diced

1 cup sliced celery

2 cloves garlic, minced

1 can (28 ounces) crushed tomatoes

1 can (15 ounces) red kidney beans, drained

1 can (14 ounces) stewed tomatoes, diced

1 to 2 tablespoons chopped pickled jalapeños

1½ to 2 tablespoons chili powder

1 tablespoon dried oregano

2 teaspoons ground cumin

1 teaspoon paprika

1 teaspoon salt

½ teaspoon black pepper

2 teaspoons bottled red hot sauce

IN A LARGE saucepan, heat the oil. Add the onion, green and red bell peppers, celery, and garlic and cook, stirring, for 6 to 7 minutes over medium heat. Add the crushed tomatoes, beans, stewed tomatoes, pickled jalapeños, chili powder, oregano, cumin, paprika, salt, black pepper, and hot sauce and bring to a simmer. Cook for 20 minutes over medium-low heat, stirring occasionally. Let stand for 5 minutes before serving.

Ladle the chili into bowls and serve at once with warm homemade corn bread.

YIELD: 4 SERVINGS

### Some Like It Hotter

ADD A FEW DASHES OF DRIED CAYENNE PEPPER AND WHITE PEPPER TO THE POT ALONG WITH THE OTHER SEASONINGS.

# Vegetarian Chili Supreme

WHOEVER SAID VEGETARIAN food isn't filling? This stick-to-your-ribs meat-less chili is sure to satisfy your appetite as well as your taste buds.

The addition of tempeh or tofu makes this dish highly nutritious. Tempeh is a processed grain-and-bean product with a chewy texture; tofu is made from processed soybeans.

1 tablespoon canola oil

1 yellow onion, diced

1 green bell pepper, seeded and diced

2 stalks celery, chopped

1 can (28 ounces) crushed tomatoes

1 can (15 ounces) red kidney beans, drained

½ pound tempeh or extra-firm tofu, diced

1 to 2 tablespoons chopped pickled jalapeños

1 tablespoon chili powder

1 tablespoon dried oregano

1½ teaspoons ground cumin

½ teaspoon black pepper

½ teaspoon salt

IN A LARGE saucepan, heat the oil. Add the onion, bell pepper, and celery and cook, stirring, over medium heat for 6 minutes. Stir in the crushed tomatoes, ⅓ cup water, the beans, tempeh, pickled jalapeños, chili powder, oregano, cumin, black pepper, and salt and bring to a simmer. Cook for 15 to 20 minutes (uncovered) over medium-low heat, stirring occasionally. Remove from the heat and let stand for 5 minutes.

Ladle the chili into bowls and serve at once with warm homemade corn bread.

YIELD: 4 TO 6 SERVINGS

🍴 *Shopping Tip*

TEMPEH AND TOFU ARE SOLD IN THE REFRIGERATOR SECTIONS OF NATURAL FOOD STORES AND SUPERMARKETS.

🌶 *Some Like It Hotter*

ADD 2 OR 3 DRIED CHILI PEPPERS (SOAKED AND MINCED) TO THE SIMMERING POT. (CHIPOTLE, CASCABEL, OR ANCHO PEPPERS ARE SOME OF MY FAVORITES.)

# Super Bowl of Red

THIS TERRIFIC CHILI is enhanced by a trio of red pepper flakes, jalapeños, and hot sauce. It makes a great party dish.

1 tablespoon canola oil

1 large yellow onion, diced

2 green or red bell peppers, seeded and diced

2 stalks celery, chopped

4 cloves garlic, minced

1 can (28 ounces) crushed tomatoes

1 can (15 ounces) red kidney beans, drained

1 to 2 tablespoons chopped pickled jalapeños

1½ tablespoons chili powder

1 tablespoon dried oregano

1½ teaspoons ground cumin

½ teaspoon red pepper flakes

½ teaspoon black pepper

½ teaspoon salt

1 to 3 teaspoons bottled red hot sauce

IN A LARGE saucepan, heat the oil. Add the onion, bell peppers, celery, and garlic and cook, stirring, for 6 minutes over medium-high heat. Stir in the crushed tomatoes, ½ cup water, the beans, pickled jalapeños, chili powder, oregano, cumin, red pepper flakes, black pepper, salt, and hot sauce and bring to a simmer. Cook for 15 to 20 minutes (uncovered) over medium-low heat, stirring occasionally. Remove from the heat and let stand for 5 to 10 minutes before serving.

Ladle the chili into bowls and serve with warm corn bread or whole wheat bread.

YIELD: 4 SERVINGS

# Cheesy Macaroni Chili

THIS RECIPE IS a playful take on another traditional American dish.

1 cup elbow macaroni

2 teaspoons canola oil

1 medium yellow onion, diced

1 green bell pepper, seeded and diced

2 stalks celery, diced

3 or 4 cloves garlic, minced

1 can (28 ounces) stewed tomatoes

1 can (15 ounces) red kidney beans, drained

1 can (11 ounces) corn kernels, drained

1½ tablespoons chili powder

2 teaspoons dried oregano

1 teaspoon ground cumin

½ teaspoon black pepper

½ teaspoon salt

½ to 1 cup shredded Monterey Jack or provolone cheese

IN A MEDIUM saucepan, bring 3 quarts of water to a boil over medium-high heat. Place the macaroni in the boiling water, stir, and return to a boil. Cook until al dente, about 6 minutes, stirring occasionally. Drain in a colander.

Meanwhile, in a large saucepan, heat the oil. Add the onion, bell pepper, celery, and garlic and cook, stirring, for 7 minutes over medium-high heat. Stir in the stewed tomatoes, beans, corn, chili powder, oregano, cumin, black pepper, and salt and bring to a simmer. Cook over medium-low heat for 15 minutes, stirring occasionally. Stir in the cooked macaroni and cook for 3 to 4 minutes over low heat. Remove from the heat and fold in the cheese. Let stand for 5 to 10 minutes before serving.

Ladle into bowls and serve with warm bread.

YIELD: 6 SERVINGS

# Cactus and Black Bean Gumbo

FRESH CACTUS PADDLES (or nopales) cook up like okra (in other words, slimy). They taste a little like green beans and make a perfect ingredient for gumbo. Cactus paddles may appear intimidating, but they are easy to prepare (be careful, though: the needles are sharp). If you can't find them, 1 cup chopped okra would be a good substitute.

1½ cups long-grain white rice
2 medium fresh cactus paddles (about ⅓ pound)
2 teaspoons canola oil
1 medium yellow onion, chopped
1 green bell pepper, seeded and diced
2 or 3 cloves garlic, minced
4 cups vegetable broth or chicken broth

1 can (15 ounces) black beans, drained
1 can (14 ounces) stewed tomatoes
2 teaspoons dried oregano
½ teaspoon dried thyme
½ teaspoon black pepper
½ teaspoon salt
¼ teaspoon cayenne pepper

IN A MEDIUM saucepan, combine the rice and 3 cups water and bring to a simmer over medium-high heat. Stir the rice, cover, and cook over medium-low heat until all of the liquid is absorbed, about 15 minutes. Fluff the grains and let stand (still covered) for 5 minutes.

Meanwhile, to prepare the cactus paddles, scrape off the prickly needles and bumps where the needles grow. Cut off the base and trim around the outer edge of the paddle. Cut the paddles in half across the width, then cut into ¼-inch-wide strips (the strips should resemble green beans). Set aside.

In another medium saucepan, heat the oil. Add the onion, bell pepper, and garlic and cook, stirring, over medium heat for about 5 minutes. Add the cactus paddles, broth, beans, stewed tomatoes, oregano, thyme, black pepper, salt, and cayenne pepper and bring to a simmer. Cook over medium heat until the cactus strips are tender, 12 to 15 minutes, stirring occasionally.

Spoon the rice into bowls and ladle the gumbo over the top. Serve at once.

YIELD: 6 SERVINGS

### Shopping Tip

FRESH CACTUS PADDLES ARE SOLD IN THE PRODUCE SECTION OF WELL-STOCKED SUPERMARKETS.

### Some Like It Hotter

ADD ½ TEASPOON WHITE PEPPER AND ¼ TEASPOON RED PEPPER FLAKES.

# Gumbo Z' Herbes

THIS MEATLESS GUMBO of greens and vegetables is served during the Lenten months in Louisiana. Legend dictates that you will make one new friend for each variety of leafy green tossed in the pot, so don't be frugal with the greens!

This gumbo is particularly good if served with Wild Pecan rice. Wild Pecan rice is neither wild nor related to pecans; however, like basmati rice, it has an intensely nutty aroma.

1 tablespoon canola oil

1 medium yellow onion, diced

1 green or red bell pepper, seeded and
    diced

1 large stalk celery, chopped

2 or 3 cloves garlic, minced

6 cups vegetable broth or water

1 can (14 ounces) stewed tomatoes

⅓ cup tomato paste

1½ teaspoons dried oregano

1 teaspoon dried thyme

½ teaspoon black pepper

½ teaspoon cayenne pepper

1 teaspoon salt

4 cups chopped leafy greens (such
    as spinach, kale, or dandelion
    greens)

¼ cup chopped fresh parsley

4 cups cooked Wild Pecan or
    basmati rice

IN A LARGE saucepan, heat the oil. Add the onion, bell pepper, celery, and garlic and cook, stirring, for 6 minutes over medium heat. Stir in the broth, stewed tomatoes, tomato paste, oregano, thyme, black pepper, cayenne pepper, and salt and bring to a simmer. Cook for 15 minutes over medium-low heat, stirring occasionally. Stir in the mixed greens and cook for about 15 minutes more. Stir in the parsley and remove from the heat.

Spoon some rice into each bowl. Ladle the gumbo over the rice and serve at once.

YIELD: 6 SERVINGS

### Some Like It Hotter

ADD A FEW DASHES OF BOTTLED HOT SAUCE TO THE GUMBO JUST BEFORE SERVING.

## Gonzo Gumbo

THIS IS A festive gumbo of crayfish, chicken, and calamari. Anything goes, of course, so try it with oysters, clams, or shrimp as well.

1 tablespoon canola oil

1 medium yellow onion, diced

1 green bell pepper, seeded and diced

2 stalks celery, chopped

4 cloves garlic, minced

½ pound boneless chicken thighs, diced

4 cups chicken broth

1 can (14 ounces) stewed tomatoes

2 teaspoons dried oregano

1½ teaspoons chili powder

½ teaspoon black pepper

½ teaspoon cayenne pepper

½ teaspoon salt

½ pound calamari, cleaned and cut into strips

½ pound frozen precooked crayfish meat, thawed

½ cup tomato paste

4 cups cooked basmati or Wild Pecan rice

IN A LARGE saucepan, heat the oil. Add the onion, bell pepper, celery, and garlic and cook, stirring, for 5 minutes over medium-high heat. Add the chicken and cook, stirring, for 5 minutes. Add the broth, stewed tomatoes, oregano, chili powder, black pepper, cayenne pepper, and salt and bring to a simmer. Stir in the calamari and crayfish and return to a simmer. Cook for 12 to 15 minutes over medium heat, stirring occasionally. Stir in the tomato paste and cook for 10 minutes over medium-low heat, stirring occasionally.

Spoon the rice into shallow bowls. Ladle the gumbo over the rice and serve at once.

YIELD: 6 SERVINGS

# Wild Mushroom and Chicken Gumbo

WOODSY WILD MUSHROOMS meld naturally into this appealing chicken gumbo.

2 tablespoons canola oil

8 ounces domestic mushrooms, sliced

4 ounces fresh shiitake or oyster
    mushrooms, sliced

1 medium yellow onion, diced

1 green bell pepper, seeded and diced

4 cloves garlic, minced

¾ pound boneless chicken breasts or
    thighs, diced

4 cups chicken broth

1 can (14 ounces) stewed tomatoes

4 whole scallions, chopped

2 teaspoons dried oregano

1 teaspoon paprika

1 teaspoon dried thyme

½ teaspoon black pepper

½ teaspoon salt

½ teaspoon cayenne pepper

4 cups cooked long-grain white,
    basmati, or Wild Pecan rice

IN A LARGE saucepan, heat the oil. Add the domestic mushrooms, shiitake mushrooms, onion, bell pepper, and garlic and cook, stirring, for 7 minutes over medium-high heat. Add the chicken and cook for 3 to 4 minutes more. Add the broth, stewed tomatoes, scallions, oregano, paprika, thyme, black pepper, salt, and cayenne pepper and bring to a simmer. Cook for 20 minutes over medium heat, stirring occasionally.

Spoon the rice into shallow bowls and ladle the gumbo over the rice. Serve with warm corn bread.

YIELD: 6 SERVINGS

## Spice Advice

SEASON THE GUMBO WITH BOTTLED RED HOT
SAUCE AND CHOPPED FRESH PARSLEY.

# Emily's Calamari Gumbo

CALAMARI, THE ITALIAN name for squid, is a natural ingredient for gumbo. This peppery bowl was my wife's inspiration.

1 tablespoon canola oil

1 medium yellow onion, diced

1 green bell pepper, seeded and diced

1 large stalk celery, chopped

4 cloves garlic, minced

4 cups chicken broth or fish stock

1 can (14 ounces) stewed tomatoes

2 teaspoons dried oregano

½ teaspoon dried thyme

½ teaspoon black pepper

½ teaspoon salt

½ teaspoon cayenne pepper

½ pound calamari, cleaned and cut
    into strips

3 tablespoons butter

3 tablespoons white flour

4 cups cooked long-grain white,
    basmati, or Wild Pecan rice

IN A LARGE saucepan, heat the oil. Add the onion, bell pepper, celery, and garlic and cook, stirring, for 7 minutes over medium-high heat. Add the broth, stewed tomatoes, oregano, thyme, black pepper, salt, and cayenne pepper and bring to a simmer. Cook over medium-low heat for 5 minutes, stirring occasionally. Stir in the calamari and cook for 15 minutes more, stirring occasionally.

Meanwhile, make the roux: Melt the butter in a small skillet over medium heat. Gradually stir in the flour, forming a paste. Cook, stirring, for 2 to 3 minutes over low heat.

When the gumbo is almost finished, whisk the roux into the broth. Continue cooking, stirring occasionally, for 1 to 2 minutes.

Spoon the rice into shallow bowls. Ladle the gumbo over the rice. Serve with warm corn bread.

YIELD: 6 SERVINGS

### ¶¶¶ Shopping Tip

CALAMARI IS AVAILABLE FRESH
OR FROZEN IN MOST WELL-
STOCKED SUPERMARKETS
AND AT FISH MARKETS.
BE SURE IT IS "CLEANED"
PRIOR TO PURCHASE.

### Some Like It Hotter

SEASON THE GUMBO WITH A
TOUCH OF BOTTLED HOT SAUCE
AND RED PEPPER FLAKES.

# Firecracker Shrimp Jambalaya

THIS JAMBALAYA WILL make your taste buds want to get up and dance!

1¼ cups long-grain white rice

1 tablespoon canola oil

1 large yellow onion, diced

1 green bell pepper, seeded and diced

2 stalks celery, diced

4 cloves garlic, minced

1 fresh cayenne chili pepper, seeded and minced

1 pound medium shrimp, peeled and deveined

1 can (28 ounces) crushed tomatoes

2 to 3 tablespoons chopped fresh parsley

2 teaspoons dried oregano

1 teaspoon ground cumin

½ teaspoon black pepper

½ teaspoon cayenne pepper

½ teaspoon salt

1 to 3 teaspoons bottled red hot sauce

IN A MEDIUM saucepan, combine the rice with 2½ cups water and bring to a simmer. Stir the grains, cover, and cook over medium-low heat until all of the liquid is absorbed, 15 to 20 minutes. Fluff the rice and set aside for 10 minutes.

Meanwhile, in a large saucepan, heat the oil. Add the onion, bell pepper, celery, garlic, and chili pepper and cook, stirring, for 5 minutes over medium heat. Stir in the shrimp and cook, stirring, for 3 to 4 minutes more. Stir in the crushed tomatoes, ½ cup water, the parsley, oregano, cumin, black pepper, cayenne pepper, salt, and hot sauce and bring to a simmer. Cook for 15 to 20 minutes over medium-low heat, stirring occasionally. Remove from the heat and fold in the rice. Let stand for 5 minutes to allow the flavors to meld together.

Ladle the jambalaya into wide bowls and serve at once.

YIELD: 4 SERVINGS

# Chorizo-Chicken Jambalaya

CHORIZO SAUSAGE IS a spicy sausage with a smoky-hot flavor. It is a perfect ingredient for this boisterous chicken jambalaya.

1¼ cups long-grain white rice

1 tablespoon canola oil

1 large yellow onion, diced

1 green bell pepper, seeded and diced

2 stalks celery, sliced

4 cloves garlic, minced

1 fresh cayenne chili pepper, seeded and minced (optional)

½ pound precooked chorizo sausage, cut into ½-inch-wide slices

¾ pound boneless chicken breasts, diced

1 can (28 ounces) crushed tomatoes

2 to 3 tablespoons chopped fresh parsley

2 teaspoons dried oregano

1 teaspoon dried thyme

½ teaspoon black pepper

½ teaspoon cayenne pepper

½ teaspoon salt

1 to 3 teaspoons bottled red hot sauce

IN A MEDIUM saucepan, combine the rice with 2½ cups water and bring to a simmer. Stir the grains, cover, and cook over medium-low heat until all of the liquid is absorbed, 15 to 20 minutes. Fluff the rice and set aside for 10 minutes.

Meanwhile, in a large saucepan, heat the oil. Add the onion, bell pepper, celery, garlic, and optional chili pepper and cook, stirring, for 5 minutes over medium heat. Stir in the sausage and chicken and cook, stirring, 5 minutes more. Stir in the crushed tomatoes, ⅓ cup water, the parsley, oregano, thyme, black pepper, cayenne pepper, salt, and hot sauce and bring to a simmer. Cook for 18 to 20 minutes over medium-low heat, stirring occasionally. Remove from the heat and fold in the rice. Let stand for 5 minutes to allow the flavors to meld together.

Ladle the jambalaya into wide bowls and serve at once.

YIELD: 4 SERVINGS

# Vegetable Jambalaya

A VEGETARIAN MASTERPIECE! Other vegetables, such as corn kernels, artichokes, or blanched broccoli florets, can be added to the simmering pot for a delicious variation. Or you can add one can (15 ounces) red kidney beans (drained) after stirring in the tomato paste and water.

1¼ cups long-grain white rice

1½ tablespoons canola oil

1 green bell pepper, seeded and diced

1 medium yellow onion, diced

1 medium zucchini, halved lengthwise and cut into ½-inch-wide slices

12 to 14 mushrooms, sliced

2 stalks celery, diced

4 cloves garlic, minced

2 cans (6 ounces each) tomato paste

¼ cup chopped fresh parsley

1 teaspoon dried basil

½ teaspoon salt

½ teaspoon black pepper

½ teaspoon cayenne pepper

IN A MEDIUM saucepan, combine the rice and 2½ cups water. Bring to a simmer over medium-high heat. Stir, cover the pan, and cook over low heat until all of the water is absorbed, about 15 minutes. Set aside.

In a large saucepan, heat the oil over medium heat. Add the bell pepper, onion, zucchini, mushrooms, celery, and garlic. Cook until the vegetables are tender, about 10 to 12 minutes, stirring frequently. Stir in the tomato paste, 2 cups water, the parsley, basil, salt, black pepper, and cayenne pepper and bring to a simmer over medium heat. Cook for 12 to 15 minutes over medium-low heat, stirring occasionally.

Fold the cooked rice into the tomato-vegetable mixture and cook for 2 to 3 minutes over low heat. Ladle into large wide bowls and serve at once.

YIELD: 4 TO 6 SERVINGS

### Some Like It Hotter

FOR A TOUCH MORE SPICE, ADD A FEW DASHES OF BOTTLED RED HOT SAUCE TO THE JAMBALAYA JUST BEFORE SERVING.

# Bourbon Street Jambalaya

———————— ❨❩ ————————

THIS BOISTEROUS JAMBALAYA is brimming with chicken, scallops, and andouille sausage—a smoky link enjoyed in many Cajun and Creole meals.

1½ cups long-grain white rice

1 tablespoon canola oil

1 medium yellow onion, diced

1 green bell pepper, seeded and diced

1 large stalk celery, diced

4 cloves garlic, minced

½ pound boneless chicken breasts, diced

½ pound sea scallops or shucked oyster meat

½ pound precooked andouille sausage, cut crosswise into ½-inch slices

2 cans (6 ounces each) tomato paste

¼ cup chopped fresh parsley

2 teaspoons dried oregano

½ teaspoon black pepper

½ teaspoon white pepper

½ teaspoon salt

¼ teaspoon cayenne pepper

IN A MEDIUM saucepan, combine the rice with 3 cups water. Bring to a simmer over medium-high heat. Stir, cover, and cook over low heat until all of the liquid is absorbed, about 15 minutes. Fluff the rice and set aside.

Meanwhile, in a large saucepan heat the oil over medium heat. Add the onion, bell pepper, celery, and garlic and cook, stirring, for 4 minutes. Add the chicken and cook, stirring, for 4 minutes more. Add the scallops and sausage and cook over medium heat until the chicken and scallops are fully cooked, about 7 to 10 minutes, stirring occasionally. Stir in the tomato paste, 2 cups water, the parsley, oregano, black pepper, white pepper, salt, and cayenne pepper and bring to a simmer. Cook for 15 minutes over low heat, stirring occasionally. Remove from the heat and fold in the rice.

Ladle into wide bowls and serve at once with warm homemade corn bread.

YIELD: 6 SERVINGS

🍴 *Shopping Tip*

ANDOUILLE SAUSAGE IS SOLD IN WELL-STOCKED SUPERMARKETS AND BUTCHER SHOPS. IF UNAVAILABLE, TRY CHORIZO OR ANOTHER SPICY SAUSAGE.

🦎 *Some Like It Hotter*

DRIZZLE SOME BOTTLED RED HOT SAUCE OVER THE JAMBALAYA JUST BEFORE SERVING.

# Catfish Creole Stew

CATFISH, THE TREASURED fish of the Deep South, is simmered in a piquant Creole tomato sauce. Ladle the stew over a bowl of rice and pass the hot sauce!

| | |
|---|---|
| 2 tablespoons canola oil | ½ teaspoon dried thyme |
| 1 medium yellow onion, diced | ½ teaspoon black pepper |
| 1 green bell pepper, seeded and diced | ½ teaspoon cayenne pepper |
| 2 stalks celery, chopped | ½ teaspoon salt |
| 4 cloves garlic, minced | 2 teaspoons bottled red hot sauce |
| 1 can (14 ounces) stewed tomatoes | 1½ pounds boneless catfish fillets, |
| 1 can (14 ounces) crushed tomatoes | coarsely chopped |
| 2 teaspoons dried oregano | 4 cups cooked long-grain white, |
| ½ teaspoon dried basil | basmati, or Wild Pecan rice |

IN A LARGE saucepan, heat 1 tablespoon of the oil. Add the onion, bell pepper, celery, and garlic and cook, stirring, for 6 minutes over medium-high heat. Add the stewed tomatoes, crushed tomatoes, oregano, basil, thyme, black pepper, cayenne pepper, salt, and hot sauce and bring to a simmer. Cook over medium-low heat for 15 minutes, stirring occasionally.

Meanwhile, in a large nonstick skillet, heat the remaining 1 tablespoon oil. Stir in the catfish and cook, stirring, over medium-high heat until the catfish is cooked in the center and opaque, about 7 minutes. Fold the fish into the sauce and return to a gentle simmer.

Spoon the rice into shallow bowls and ladle the stew over the rice. Serve with corn bread.

YIELD: 4 SERVINGS

# Pan-Seared Creole Scallops

---

LARGE SEA SCALLOPS are able to absorb the spicy kinetic flavors of this Creole sauce.

| | |
|---|---|
| 2 tablespoons canola oil | ½ teaspoon dried basil |
| 1 medium yellow onion, diced | ½ teaspoon dried thyme |
| 1 green bell pepper, seeded and diced | ½ teaspoon black pepper |
| | ½ teaspoon salt |
| 2 stalks celery, chopped | ½ teaspoon cayenne pepper |
| 4 cloves garlic, minced | 2 teaspoons bottled red hot sauce |
| 1 can (14 ounces) stewed tomatoes | 1½ pounds sea scallops |
| 1 can (14 ounces) crushed tomatoes | 4 cups cooked long-grain white, |
| 2 teaspoons dried oregano | basmati, or Wild Pecan rice |

IN A LARGE saucepan, heat 1 tablespoon of the oil. Add the onion, bell pepper, celery, and garlic and cook, stirring, for 7 minutes over medium-high heat. Add the stewed tomatoes, crushed tomatoes, oregano, basil, thyme, black pepper, salt, cayenne pepper, and hot sauce and bring to a simmer. Cook over medium-low heat for 15 minutes, stirring occasionally.

Meanwhile, in a large nonstick skillet, heat the remaining 1 tablespoon oil. Stir in the scallops and cook, stirring, over medium-high heat until the shellfish are opaque and firm, 7 to 10 minutes. Fold the scallops into the sauce and return to a simmer.

Spoon the rice into shallow bowls and ladle the scallops and sauce over the rice. Serve with corn bread.

YIELD: 4 SERVINGS

# CHAPTER FIVE

# Sopa, Locro, and Pozole

## SOUPS AND STEWS FROM MEXICO TO SOUTH AMERICA

HUNDREDS OF YEARS ago, long before Christopher Columbus arrived in the New World, the ancient Mayans and Aztecs of Mexico and Incas of South America had discovered the joy of chili peppers. Along with corn, pumpkin, tomatoes, and cocoa, a variety of chili peppers have been cultivated and revered for centuries. Although the spicy soups and stews of the sprawling region have different names (sopa, chupe, locro, and sancocho, to name a few), the common link is a fondness for chili peppers.

Mexico has often been called the chili capital of the world—and for a good reason. There are scores of exotic chili peppers used in Mexican cooking, from the versatile **green jalapeño** and piercing **serrano** to the mellifluous **poblano**, woodsy **cascabel**, smoky **chipotle**, raisiny **ancho**, slender **guajillo**, and roaring **habanero**. A plethora of fresh and dried chilies with vibrant personas provide the essential flavors of Mexican cuisine.

To the misinformed or misguided, Mexican food is unfairly perceived as a heaping plate of tacos, nachos, and refried beans. To the contrary, aficionados of south-of-the-border cooking can attest to the diverse, eclectic, and alluring tastes of Mexican cuisine. From Green Pozole Stew, Cactus Paddle and Pasta Soup, and Serrano Pilaf to Mexicali Black Bean Soup and Cascabel Potato Soup, authentic Mexican fare is a carnival of exciting flavors and aromas waiting to be explored.

While Mexico is the undisputed chili capital of the world, South America is regarded as the birthplace of the pungent pods. Experts have placed the origin of the chili peppers near the Amazon jungles of Bolivia and Brazil in the heart of the continent. Of course, many contemporary South American meals are invigorated with the fiery chili peppers. Recipes include Locro Chicken, a country stew; Porotos Granados ("grand beans"), a festive bowl of corn and beans; and Coastal Chilean Fish Stew, a pot-au-feu–style hot pot. The famous Brazilian Feijoada, a boisterous black bean stew served with rice and braised greens, is also enlightened with fresh chilies.

Although some virulent varieties of popular South American chilies have not arrived en masse in the United States, their reputation precedes them. For example, the **rocoto,** also called manzana, is a yellowish-orange curvy pod with black seeds that is reputed to be hotter than the habanero. In Brazil, the **malagueta pepper,** a Tabasco-like chili, supplies a blistering heat to sauces, marinades, and soups. Chili connoisseurs avidly await the arrival of these intriguing chilies to American kitchens.

# Vegetable Locro

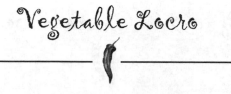

THIS STEW IS made with a South American squash called zapallo. Butternut squash or West Indian pumpkin can be used instead.

1 tablespoon canola oil

1 medium yellow onion, diced

2 or 3 cloves garlic, minced

1 or 2 jalapeño or red Fresno peppers, seeded and minced

3 or 4 tomatoes, diced

2 tablespoons dried parsley

1 tablespoon paprika

1 tablespoon dried oregano

½ teaspoon black pepper

½ teaspoon salt

4 cups peeled, diced butternut squash or West Indian pumpkin

1 can (15 ounces) corn kernels, drained

4 to 6 cups cooked long-grain white rice

IN A LARGE saucepan, heat the oil over medium heat. Add the onion, garlic, and chili peppers and cook, stirring, for 5 minutes. Add the tomatoes, parsley, paprika, oregano, black pepper, and salt and cook, stirring, for 4 to 5 minutes more. Add the squash and 3 cups water and bring to a simmer. Cook for 25 minutes over medium heat, stirring occasionally, until the squash is tender. Add the corn and cook for 5 to 10 minutes over low heat, stirring occasionally. To thicken the stew, mash the squash against the side of the pan with the back of a spoon.

Spoon the rice into large bowls and ladle the stew over the top.

YIELD: 4 TO 6 SERVINGS

# Yucatán Chicken Soup

CALLED SOPA DE LIMA, this brothy chicken soup from the Mexican peninsula has a subtle lime fragrance and peppery disposition.

| | |
|---|---|
| 1 tablespoon canola oil | 4 cups chicken broth |
| 1 large yellow onion, diced | 1½ teaspoons dried oregano |
| 3 cloves garlic, minced | ½ teaspoon black pepper |
| 2 serrano or jalapeño peppers, seeded and minced | ½ teaspoon salt |
| | 3 (6-inch) corn tortillas, cut into |
| ¾ pound boneless chicken breasts or thighs, diced | ½-inch strips |
| | Juice of 2 limes |
| 1 large tomato, diced | 2 tablespoons chopped fresh cilantro |

IN A LARGE saucepan, heat the oil. Add the onion, garlic, and chili peppers and cook, stirring, for 4 minutes over medium-high heat. Add the chicken and tomato and cook, stirring, for 4 minutes more. Add the broth, oregano, black pepper, and salt and bring to a simmer. Cook for 20 minutes over medium heat, stirring occasionally. Stir in the tortilla strips and lime juice and cook for 3 minutes more. Stir in the cilantro.

Ladle the soup into bowls and serve at once.

YIELD: 4 SERVINGS

### Some Like It Hotter

THE FIERY HABANERO PEPPER IS NATIVE TO THE YUCATÁN AND CAN BE USED IN PLACE OF THE SERRANO CHILIES. USE ABOUT HALF A HABANERO PEPPER IN THIS RECIPE.

# Sopa de Fideo (Mexican Noodle Soup)

THIS WHOLESOME NOODLE soup is laden with vegetables, aromatic spices, and feisty chilies—a sort of Mexican minestrone.

| | |
|---|---|
| 1 tablespoon canola oil | 2 carrots, diced |
| 1 medium yellow onion, diced | 1 can (14 ounces) stewed tomatoes |
| 1 large red or green bell pepper, seeded and diced | 1 tablespoon dried oregano |
| | 2 teaspoons ground cumin |
| 2 stalks celery, chopped | 1 teaspoon salt |
| 3 or 4 cloves garlic, minced | ½ teaspoon black pepper |
| 2 jalapeño or serrano chilies, seeded and minced | 4 ounces angel hair pasta |
| | ¼ cup chopped fresh parsley |
| 8 cups vegetable broth or water | ½ cup shredded Monterey Jack cheese |
| 1 large potato, diced | |

IN A LARGE saucepan, heat the oil. Add the onion, bell pepper, celery, garlic, and chili peppers and cook, stirring, for 7 minutes over medium heat. Add the broth, potato, carrots, stewed tomatoes, oregano, cumin, salt, and black pepper and bring to a simmer. Cook for 20 to 25 minutes over medium-low heat, stirring occasionally.

Snap the pasta in half and stir into the soup. Cook over medium heat until the pasta is al dente, about 4 minutes. Stir in the parsley and let the soup stand for a few minutes before serving.

Ladle the soup into bowls and top with shredded cheese. Serve the bowls of soup with warm flour tortillas.

YIELD: 6 SERVINGS

# Macho Gazpacho

HERE'S A COOL bowl with hot flavors. This summertime soup, sometimes called a "liquid salad," includes garden vegetables, tomatoes, garlic, and hot peppers.

Garnish the gazpacho with a colorful mix of chopped cucumbers, onions, and fresh parsley.

| | |
|---|---|
| 2 medium tomatoes, diced | 2 tablespoons chopped fresh parsley |
| 1 small red onion, chopped | 1 teaspoon bottled red hot sauce |
| 1 Italian sweet pepper, seeded and diced | ½ teaspoon ground cumin |
| | ½ teaspoon black pepper |
| 1 cucumber, peeled and diced | ½ teaspoon salt |
| 1 to 2 tablespoons minced pickled jalapeños | ¼ teaspoon red pepper flakes |
| | 2 cups canned tomato juice |
| 2 cloves garlic, minced | (preferably low sodium) |

IN A LARGE mixing bowl, combine all of the ingredients. Place three-quarters of the mixture in a blender or food processor fitted with a steel blade and process for about 5 seconds, forming a vegetable mash. Return to the bowl and blend with the remaining vegetable mixture. Chill for 30 minutes to 1 hour before serving.

Ladle the gazpacho into chilled bowls and serve with crusty French bread.

YIELD: 4 SERVINGS

## ✕ Spice Advice

SERVE IT WITH A COOL YOGURT
CONDIMENT, SUCH AS RAITA
OR PLAIN LOWFAT YOGURT,
FOR A NICE CONTRAST IN
TEXTURE AND FLAVOR.

## ◗ Some Like It Hotter

SERVE A BOTTLE OF RED HOT
SAUCE ON THE SIDE FOR THOSE
WHO LIKE IT HOTTER.

# Cascabel Potato Soup

CASCABEL CHILIES HAVE a dark mahogany hue and a bulbous shape (*cascabel* means "rattle" or "jingle"—the seeds inside the pods make a rattling sound when shaken). They imbue this potato and cheese bisque with a smoky flavor and medium heat.

4 to 6 dried cascabel chilies

1 cup simmering water

1 tablespoon canola oil

1 medium yellow onion, diced

2 red bell peppers, seeded and diced

3 or 4 cloves garlic, minced

4 cups chicken broth or water

2½ cups peeled, diced potatoes

1 large carrot, diced

½ teaspoon white pepper

½ teaspoon salt

1 cup light cream or milk

½ pound shredded Monterey Jack cheese

2 tablespoons chopped fresh cilantro (optional)

COVER THE CHILIES with the simmering water and soak until soft, about 15 to 20 minutes. Place a lid or plate over the chilies to keep them from floating. Drain the chilies, remove the seeds, and chop the flesh. Set aside.

In a large saucepan, heat the oil. Add the onion, bell peppers, and garlic and cook, stirring, for about 6 minutes over medium-high heat. Add the broth, potatoes, carrot, white pepper, salt, and chilies and bring to a simmer. Cook over medium-low heat until the potatoes are tender, about 20 minutes, stirring occasionally.

Transfer the soup to a food processor fitted with a steel blade or to a blender and process until smooth, about 5 seconds. Return to the pan and stir in the cream, cheese, and optional cilantro. Return to a gentle simmer over medium-low heat.

Ladle the bisque into bowls and serve at once.

Y<small>IELD</small>: 6 <small>SERVINGS</small>

✂ *Spice Advice*

O<small>THER DRIED CHILIES, SUCH AS PASILLA, ANCHO, OR GUAJILLO, CAN ALSO BE USED (ONLY TWO OR THREE OF THE LARGER CHILIES ARE NEEDED).</small>

# Vegetable Tortilla Soup

MIXED VEGETABLES, CHILIES, corn, and tortillas fill this bowl, known as sopa de tortilla.

1 tablespoon canola oil

1 medium yellow onion, diced

1 small zucchini, diced

1 red bell pepper, seeded and diced

2 cloves garlic, minced

1 or 2 jalapeño or serrano peppers, seeded and minced

6 cups vegetable stock or chicken broth

1 can (14 ounces) stewed tomatoes

2 teaspoons dried oregano

1½ teaspoons ground cumin

1 teaspoon salt

1 can (14 ounces) corn kernels, drained

4 (6-inch) flour tortillas, cut into ½-inch strips

½ to 1 cup shredded Monterey Jack cheese

IN A LARGE saucepan, heat the oil. Add the onion, zucchini, bell pepper, garlic, and chili peppers and cook, stirring, for 5 to 7 minutes over medium heat. Add the stock, stewed tomatoes, oregano, cumin, and salt and bring to a simmer. Cook for 15 minutes over medium-low heat, stirring occasionally. Stir in the corn and tortilla strips and cook for 10 minutes more. Let stand for 5 minutes before serving.

Ladle the soup into bowls and sprinkle with cheese.

YIELD: 6 SERVINGS

### Some Like It Hotter

ADD 2 ROASTED POBLANO CHILIES (CHOPPED) AND 2 TABLESPOONS MINCED CILANTRO TO THE SIMMERING BROTH.

# Mexicali Black Bean Soup

THIS QUINTESSENTIAL, easy-to-prepare black bean soup is perfect for any time of year.

1 tablespoon canola oil

1 medium yellow onion, diced

1 green bell pepper, seeded and diced

2 stalks celery, chopped

2 cans (15 ounces each) black beans

1 cup canned crushed tomatoes

1 cup water or vegetable broth

2 to 3 tablespoons chopped fresh parsley

1 to 2 tablespoons chopped pickled jalapeños

1 tablespoon chili powder

2 teaspoons dried oregano

1½ teaspoons ground cumin

½ teaspoon salt

2 or 3 tablespoons chopped fresh cilantro

IN A LARGE saucepan, heat the oil. Add the onion, bell pepper, and celery and cook, stirring, for 5 minutes over medium heat. Add the black beans, crushed tomatoes, water, parsley, pickled jalapeños, chili powder, oregano, cumin, and salt and bring to a simmer. Cook for 15 minutes over medium-low heat, stirring occasionally. Transfer about half of the soup to a blender or a food processor fitted with a steel blade and puree until smooth, about 5 seconds. Return the pureed soup to the pan and stir in the cilantro. Ladle the soup into bowls and serve at once.

YIELD: 4 SERVINGS

**Spice Advice**

PLAIN LOWFAT YOGURT MAKES A SOOTHING TOPPING.

# Cactus Paddle and Pasta Soup

AFTER CORN, CACTUS paddles (called nopales) are Mexico's most popular vegetable. When cut into strips, they have a flavor like green beans and a texture like okra (be careful, though: the needles are sharp).

2 medium fresh cactus paddles (about ⅓ pound)

2 teaspoons canola oil

1 medium yellow onion, diced

1 zucchini, diced

2 or 3 cloves garlic, minced

4 cups vegetable broth

1 can (14 ounces) stewed tomatoes

1 medium potato, diced

1 tablespoon chopped pickled jalapeños

2 teaspoons dried oregano

1 teaspoon dried basil

½ teaspoon black pepper

½ teaspoon salt

½ cup tomato paste

⅓ cup tiny pasta (such as tubettini or ditalini)

To PREPARE THE cactus paddles, scrape off the prickly needles and bumps where the needles grow. Cut off the base and trim around the outer edge of the paddle. Cut the paddles in half across the width, then cut into ¼-inch-wide strips (the strips should resemble green beans). Set aside.

In a large saucepan, heat the oil over medium heat. Add the onion, zucchini, and garlic and cook, stirring, until the onion is translucent, about 5 minutes. Add the broth, stewed tomatoes, potato, pickled jalapeños, oregano, basil, black pepper, and salt and bring to a simmer. Cook for 10 minutes over medium heat, stirring occasionally. Stir in the cactus paddles, tomato paste, and pasta and cook until the nopales and potatoes are tender, about 10 to 15 minutes, stirring occasionally. Let stand for 5 minutes before serving.

Ladle the soup into bowls and serve at once with plenty of warm flour tortillas.

YIELD: 6 SERVINGS

𝗬𝗜 Shopping Tip

FRESH CACTUS PADDLES
ARE SOLD IN THE PRODUCE
SECTION OF WELL-STOCKED
SUPERMARKETS.

Some Like It Hotter

ADD 2 CANNED CHIPOTLE
PEPPERS (SEEDED AND MINCED)
TO THE SIMMERING POT.

# Well-Cooked "Olla" Beans

In Mexico, a variety of beans are cooked in a large, earthenware bean pot called an olla. The bean chili-stew is often served as a spicy side dish. Remember to always soak dried beans in plenty of water before cooking; after draining, cook the beans in fresh water.

1½ cups dried black beans, soaked
    overnight and drained
1 tablespoon canola oil
1 medium yellow onion, diced
1 red bell pepper, seeded and diced
2 stalks celery, chopped
3 or 4 cloves garlic, minced
2 jalapeño or serrano peppers, seeded
    and minced

¼ cup tomato paste
¼ cup chopped fresh
    parsley
1 tablespoon chili powder
2 teaspoons dried oregano
1 teaspoon ground cumin
1 teaspoon ground coriander
1 teaspoon salt
½ teaspoon black pepper

In a large saucepan, combine the beans and 7 to 8 cups water and bring to a simmer. Cook over medium-low heat until tender, about 1½ hours. Drain the beans, reserving 2 cups of the cooking liquid.

In a large saucepan, heat the oil. Add the onion, bell pepper, celery, garlic, and chili peppers and cook, stirring, for 5 minutes over medium heat. Add the beans with their cooking liquid, the tomato paste, parsley, chili powder, oregano, cumin, coriander, salt, and black pepper and bring to a simmer. Cook for 10 to 15 minutes over medium-low heat, stirring occasionally.

To thicken, transfer about one-third of the beans to a blender or food processor fitted with a steel blade and process until smooth, about 5 seconds. Return the pureed beans to the pan.

Ladle the beans into bowls and serve with warm flour tortillas.

Yield: 6 servings

### Some Like It Hotter

Add 1 habanero pepper (seeded and minced) along with the other chili peppers.

# Pozole Rojo (Red Posole)

POZOLE (OR POSOLE) is a Mexican chili-stew made with chewy corn kernels (the corn is also called posole, or hominy). This meatless version is loaded with beans, tomatoes, and pureed dried chilies.

3 or 4 dried Mexican chilies (such as
    guajillo or ancho), seeded

1 cup simmering water

1 tablespoon canola oil

1 medium yellow onion, diced

1 red bell pepper, seeded and diced

2 large cloves garlic, minced

1 can (28 ounces) tomato puree

1 can (15 ounces) corn hominy,
    drained

1 can (15 ounces) red kidney beans,
    drained

1 can (14 ounces) stewed tomatoes

1 tablespoon dried oregano

2 teaspoons ground cumin

½ teaspoon salt

HEAT AN UNGREASED skillet and add the chilies. Cook over medium heat until lightly toasted, about 2 minutes. Shake the pan and turn the chilies as they cook. Remove from the heat and cover the chilies with the simmering water. Soak for 15 to 20 minutes. Place a lid or plate over the chilies to keep them from floating. Add the chilies and about ½ cup soaking liquid to a blender or a food processor fitted with a steel blade and process until smooth, about 5 seconds. Scrape the pureed chilies into a small bowl and set aside.

In a large saucepan, heat the oil. Add the onion, bell pepper, and garlic and cook, stirring, for 6 minutes over medium heat. Stir in the tomato puree, hominy, beans, stewed tomatoes, oregano, cumin, salt, and pureed chilies and bring to a simmer. Cook for 15 to 20 minutes over medium-low heat, stirring occasionally.

Remove the posole from the heat and let stand for 5 minutes before serving. Ladle the posole into bowls and serve with warm flour tortillas.

YIELD: 6 SERVINGS

### 🍴 Shopping Tip

HOMINY IS AVAILABLE EITHER CANNED OR FROZEN IN WELL-STOCKED GROCERY STORES. DRIED MEXICAN CHILIES SUCH AS GUAJILLO AND ANCHO ARE AVAILABLE IN WELL-STOCKED SUPERMARKETS AND MEXICAN GROCERY STORES.

# Locro Chicken

LOCRO IS A one-pot stew enjoyed throughout Central and South America. This bountiful version is sated with chicken, tomatoes, squash, and hot peppers.

1 tablespoon canola oil

1 medium yellow onion, diced

1 red bell pepper, seeded and diced

4 cloves garlic, minced

2 jalapeño or red Fresno peppers,
    seeded and minced

1 can (14 ounces) stewed tomatoes

¾ pound boneless chicken thighs, diced

1 tablespoon dried parsley

1 tablespoon paprika

1 tablespoon dried oregano

1 teaspoon salt

½ teaspoon black pepper

3½ cups chicken broth or water

2 cups peeled, diced winter squash
    (such as butternut or Hubbard)

1½ cups long-grain white rice

4 whole scallions, chopped

IN A LARGE saucepan, heat the oil. Add the onion, bell pepper, garlic, and chili peppers and cook, stirring, for 5 minutes over medium heat. Add the tomatoes, chicken, parsley, paprika, oregano, salt, and black pepper and cook, stirring, for 5 minutes more. Stir in the broth, squash, and rice and bring to a simmer. Cover and cook over medium heat until the squash and rice are tender, about 20 minutes, stirring occasionally.

Remove from the heat, fluff the grains, and fold in the scallions. Let stand (covered) for about 5 minutes before serving.

Spoon the stew into wide bowls and serve at once with braised greens or a leafy salad on the side.

YIELD: 4 SERVINGS

*Some Like It Hotter*

DRIZZLE A FEW DROPS OF HABANERO HOT SAUCE INTO THE POT JUST BEFORE SERVING.

119

# Borracho Beans

BLACK BEANS AND red beans are simmered with beer, roasted chilies, and assertive spices (*borracho* means "drunken" in Spanish). Serve this as a hearty side dish.

2 or 3 poblano or fresh New Mexico
    chilies, cored and seeded

1 tablespoon canola oil

1 medium yellow onion, diced

1 large stalk celery, chopped

2 large cloves garlic, minced

1 can (15 ounces) black beans

1 can (15 ounces) red kidney beans

1 can (14 ounces) stewed
    tomatoes

1 medium potato, diced

½ cup stale beer

1 tablespoon dried oregano

2 teaspoons chili powder

1½ teaspoons ground cumin

½ teaspoon black pepper

TO ROAST THE chilies, place the pods over a hot grill or beneath a pre-heated broiler for 4 to 5 minutes on each side until the skin is charred. Remove from the heat and let cool for a few minutes. Using a butter knife, peel off the charred skin and discard. Finely chop the flesh.

In a large saucepan, heat the oil. Add the onion, celery, and garlic and cook, stirring, for 5 minutes over medium heat. Add the black beans, kidney beans, stewed tomatoes, potato, beer, ½ cup water, the oregano, chili powder, cumin, black pepper, and roasted chilies and bring to a simmer. Cook over medium heat until the potato is tender, about 20 minutes, stirring occasionally.

Ladle the bean stew into bowls and serve at once.

YIELD: 6 SERVINGS

# Brazilian Feijoada

THIS ROBUST VERSION of the venerated Brazilian black bean stew is heightened with smoky chipotle peppers and spicy chorizo sausages. Cooked white rice and braised leafy greens are the traditional accompaniments for this dish.

1 tablespoon canola oil

1 medium yellow onion, diced

1 red bell pepper, seeded and diced

4 cloves garlic, minced

½ pound sirloin or top round, cubed

½ pound precooked chorizo sausage, sliced

2 cans (15 ounces each) black beans

1 cup chicken broth

1 or 2 canned chipotle peppers, minced

3 to 4 tablespoons chopped fresh parsley

2 teaspoons chili powder

1 teaspoon dried thyme

1 teaspoon dried oregano

½ teaspoon black pepper

½ teaspoon salt

¼ cup tomato paste

IN A LARGE saucepan, heat the oil. Add the onion, bell pepper, and garlic and cook, stirring, for 4 minutes over medium-high heat. Add the beef and chorizo and cook, stirring, for 7 minutes. Stir in the beans with their liquid. Add the broth, chipotle pepper, parsley, chili powder, thyme, oregano, black pepper, and salt and bring to a simmer. Cook for 10 minutes over medium-low heat, stirring occasionally. Stir in the tomato paste and cook for 10 minutes over low heat, stirring occasionally. Let stand for 5 minutes before serving.

Ladle the stew into large, shallow bowls and serve at once.

YIELD: 4 SERVINGS

# Coastal Chilean Fish Stew

CALLED CALDITO DE PESCADO, this ocean stew is brimming with potatoes, carrots, white beans, seafood, and radiant chilies.

| | |
|---|---|
| 1 tablespoon canola oil | 1 teaspoon salt |
| 2 stalks celery, chopped | ½ teaspoon dried thyme |
| 2 carrots, diced | ½ teaspoon black pepper |
| 1 cup chopped leeks | ½ pound marlin or swordfish steaks, |
| 4 cloves garlic, minced | cubed |
| 2 jalapeño or serrano peppers, seeded | ¼ pound clam strips or oyster meat |
| and minced | 1 can (14 ounces) stewed tomatoes |
| 5 cups water or fish stock | 1 can (15 ounces) white kidney |
| 2 medium potatoes, peeled and diced | beans, drained |
| 2 teaspoons dried oregano | 1 cup light cream |

IN A LARGE saucepan, heat the oil. Add the celery, carrots, leeks, garlic, and chili peppers and cook, stirring, for 5 minutes over medium-high heat. Add the water, potatoes, oregano, salt, thyme, and black pepper and bring to a simmer. Cook for 15 minutes over medium heat, stirring occasionally. Add the seafood, stewed tomatoes, and beans and return to a simmer. Cook for 15 minutes more, stirring occasionally. Stir in the cream and return to a gentle simmer over medium-low heat.

Remove the stew from the heat and let stand for 5 to 10 minutes before serving. Ladle into large bowls and serve with warm crusty bread.

YIELD: 8 SERVINGS

# Fisherman's Chili Stew

INSPIRED BY THE Chilean stew called mariscado, this tomato-based fish stew is an aromatic and piquant cousin to Manhattan fish chowder.

1 tablespoon canola oil

1 medium yellow onion, diced

1 green bell pepper, seeded and diced

2 stalks celery, chopped

4 cloves garlic, minced

2 jalapeño or serrano peppers, seeded and minced

2 cups clam juice

2 cups diced potatoes

1 can (14 ounces) stewed tomatoes

2 teaspoons dried oregano

1 teaspoon dried thyme

½ teaspoon black pepper

½ teaspoon salt

½ pound medium shrimp, peeled and deveined

½ pound oyster meat or clam strips

½ pound boneless white fish fillets (such as cod or sole), cubed

½ cup tomato paste

IN A LARGE saucepan, heat the oil. Add the onion, bell pepper, celery, garlic, and chili peppers and cook, stirring, for 6 minutes over medium-high heat. Add 4 cups water, the clam juice, potatoes, stewed tomatoes, oregano, thyme, black pepper, and salt and bring to a simmer. Cook for 10 minutes over medium heat, stirring occasionally.

Stir in the shrimp, oysters, and fish fillets and return to a simmer. Cook for 15 to 20 minutes over medium heat, stirring occasionally. Stir in the tomato paste and cook for 5 to 10 minutes more.

Ladle the stew into shallow bowls and serve with warm bread.

YIELD: 8 SERVINGS

*Shopping Tip*

CLAM JUICE IS AVAILABLE IN MOST SUPERMARKETS.

# Green Pozole Stew

---

TOMATILLOS, PORK, HERBS, and green chilies fill this traditional Mexican stew with enticing flavors and textures.

Tomatillos are green tomato-like fruits with thin husks and a mildly sour flavor. If using fresh tomatillos, blanch them in boiling water for 10 minutes before adding to the recipe.

2 tablespoons canola oil

¾ pound boneless pork loin,
   diced

1 medium yellow onion, diced

1 green bell pepper, seeded and diced

2 stalks celery, chopped

4 cloves garlic, minced

2 serrano or jalapeño peppers, seeded
   and minced

1 can (15 ounces) crushed tomatoes

1 can (14 ounces) corn hominy,
   drained

1 can (14 ounces) stewed tomatoes

1 can (12 ounces) tomatillos, drained
   and diced

1 tablespoon dried oregano

½ teaspoon black pepper

½ teaspoon salt

IN A WIDE skillet, heat 1 tablespoon of the oil. Add the pork and cook, stirring, over medium-high heat until browned, about 7 minutes. Set aside.

In a large saucepan, heat the remaining 1 tablespoon oil. Add the onion, bell pepper, celery, garlic, and chili peppers and cook, stirring, for 5 to 7 minutes over medium-high heat. Stir in the crushed tomatoes, hominy, stewed tomatoes, tomatillos, oregano, black pepper, salt, and pork and bring to a simmer. Cook for 15 to 20 minutes over medium-low heat, stirring occasionally. Remove from the heat and let stand for 5 minutes before serving.

Ladle the posole into bowls and serve at once with plenty of warm flour tortillas.

YIELD: 4 SERVINGS

🍴 *Shopping Tip*

CANNED TOMATILLOS ARE
SOLD AT WELL-STOCKED
SUPERMARKETS.

✗ *Spice Advice*

ADD 2 OR 3 TABLESPOONS
OF CHOPPED FRESH CILANTRO
TO THE STEW A FEW MINUTES
BEFORE SERVING.

# Sirloin Chili Colorado

ANCHO AND GUAJILLO chilies, two popular chilies in Mexico, imbue this cauldron with warm, endearing flavors. "Colorado" refers to the red hue of the dish.

Tougher cuts of beef, such as top round or sirloin tip, can also be used, but they should be diced into smaller pieces.

| | |
|---|---|
| 2 or 3 ancho or guajillo chilies | 1 can (15 ounces) black beans |
| 1 cup simmering water | 1 can (28 ounces) crushed |
| 1 tablespoon canola oil | tomatoes |
| 1 medium yellow onion, diced | 1½ tablespoons chili powder |
| 1 red bell pepper, seeded and diced | 1 tablespoon dried oregano |
| 2 stalks celery, chopped | 1½ teaspoons ground |
| 4 cloves garlic, minced | cumin |
| ¾ pound boneless top sirloin or strip | ½ teaspoon salt |
| loin steak, cubed | ½ teaspoon cayenne pepper |

HEAT AN UNGREASED skillet and add the chilies. Cook over medium heat until the chilies are lightly toasted, about 2 minutes, shaking the pan and turning the pods as they cook. Remove from the heat and cover with the simmering water. Soak for 15 minutes. Place a lid or plate over the chilies to keep them from floating. Transfer the chilies and ½ cup soaking liquid to a blender and process until pureed, about 5 seconds. Scrape the pureed chilies into a small bowl.

In a large saucepan, heat the oil. Add the onion, bell pepper, celery, and garlic and cook, stirring, for 6 minutes over medium heat. Stir in the beef and cook, stirring, for 3 to 4 minutes more. Add the beans with their liquid, the crushed tomatoes, chili powder, oregano, cumin, salt, and cayenne pepper and bring to a simmer. Cook for 15 minutes over medium-low heat, stirring occasionally. Stir in the pureed chilies and cook for about 5 minutes more.

Ladle the chili into bowls and serve at once with warm homemade corn bread.

YIELD: 6 SERVINGS

*Shopping Tip*

A VARIETY OF DRIED CHILI PEPPERS ARE AVAILABLE IN MOST WELL-STOCKED SUPERMARKETS.

# Porotos Granados

PUMPKIN, CORN, AND beans (nicknamed "the three sisters") have been grown together for centuries in pre-Columbian America. In Chile, this trio inspires a stew called porotos granados ("grand beans").

1 tablespoon canola oil

1 medium yellow onion, diced

3 or 4 cloves garlic, minced

2 jalapeño peppers, seeded and minced

2 large tomatoes, diced

1 tablespoon paprika

1 tablespoon dried oregano

1 tablespoon dried parsley

1 teaspoon ground cumin

½ teaspoon black pepper

½ teaspoon salt

4 cups peeled, diced pumpkin, red kuri, or butternut squash

1 can (15 ounces) corn kernels, drained

1 can (15 ounces) cranberry beans or Roman beans, drained

IN A LARGE saucepan, heat the oil. Add the onion, garlic, and jalapeño peppers and cook, stirring, for 4 minutes over medium heat. Add the tomatoes, paprika, oregano, parsley, cumin, black pepper, and salt and cook, stirring, for 3 to 4 minutes more. Add the pumpkin and 2¼ cups water and bring to a simmer. Cook over medium heat until the pumpkin is tender, about 25 minutes, stirring occasionally. Stir in the corn and beans and cook for about 10 minutes more over low heat. To thicken, mash the pumpkin against the side of the pan with the back of a large spoon.

Ladle the stew into wide bowls over a bed of quinoa or rice. Serve at once.

YIELD: 4 SERVINGS

🍴 Shopping Tip

RED KURI SQUASH IS AVAILABLE
IN AUTUMN AT FARMERS'
MARKETS AND WELL-STOCKED
SUPERMARKETS. CRANBERRY
AND ROMAN BEANS ARE
AVAILABLE IN THE
CANNED BEAN SECTION OF
MOST SUPERMARKETS.

# Chipotle-Spiced Chicken with Lentils

THE EARTHY FLAVOR of stewed lentils melds wonderfully with the chipotle-enhanced chicken.

2 tablespoons canola oil

1 medium yellow onion, diced

1 large stalk celery, chopped

4 cloves garlic, minced

1 cup green lentils, rinsed

2 cups diced sweet potatoes

1 teaspoon ground cumin

1 teaspoon ground coriander

½ teaspoon black pepper

½ pound boneless chicken breasts, diced

1 or 2 canned chipotle peppers, minced

¼ cup chopped fresh parsley

1 teaspoon salt

IN A LARGE saucepan, heat 1 tablespoon of the oil. Add the onion, celery, and garlic and cook, stirring, for 5 minutes over medium-high heat. Stir in the lentils and 7 cups water and bring to a simmer. Cook for 10 minutes over medium heat, stirring occasionally. Stir in the sweet potatoes, cumin, coriander, and black pepper and cook until the lentils are tender, about 25 minutes, stirring occasionally.

Meanwhile, in a wide skillet, heat the remaining 1 tablespoon oil. Add the chicken and cook, stirring, over medium heat until browned, about 7 minutes. Stir in the chipotle pepper, parsley, and salt and cook, stirring, for 2 minutes more.

When the lentils are tender, add the chicken mixture and cook, stirring, for about 5 minutes more over medium heat.

Ladle the stew into bowls and serve at once with plenty of warm flour tortillas.

YIELD: 6 SERVINGS

### 🍴 Shopping Tip

CANNED CHIPOTLE CHILIES IN ADOBO SAUCE ARE AVAILABLE AT WELL-STOCKED SUPERMARKETS AND AT MEXICAN GROCERY STORES. OTHER DRIED PEPPERS CAN BE USED BUT MUST BE REHYDRATED PRIOR TO COOKING.

### 🌶 Some Like It Hotter

ADD 1 OR 2 SERRANO PEPPERS (SEEDED AND MINCED) TO THE PAN ALONG WITH THE CHIPOTLE PEPPERS.

# Green Poblano, Rice, and Beans

ARROZ VERDE, OR green rice, is a Mexican pilaf loaded with green vegetables, herbs, and chilies.

| | |
|---|---|
| 2 or 3 poblano chilies, cored and seeded | 1 cup cooked or (drained) canned |
| 1 tablespoon canola oil | black beans or pinto beans |
| 1 medium yellow onion, diced | 1½ teaspoons ground cumin |
| 8 ounces mushrooms, chopped | 1 teaspoon salt |
| 3 or 4 cloves garlic, minced | ½ teaspoon black pepper |
| 2½ cups chopped fresh spinach | ¼ cup chopped fresh parsley |
| 3¼ cups water or chicken broth | 4 whole scallions, trimmed and |
| 1½ cups long-grain white rice | chopped |

To ROAST THE chilies, place the pods over a hot grill or beneath a preheated broiler for 4 to 5 minutes on each side until the skin is charred. Remove from the heat and let cool for a few minutes. Using a butter knife, peel off the charred skin and discard. Finely chop the flesh.

In a medium saucepan, heat the oil. Add the onion, mushrooms, and garlic and cook, stirring, for 5 minutes over medium heat. Stir in the spinach and cook, stirring, until the leaves are wilted, about 2 minutes. Stir in the water, rice, beans, cumin, salt, black pepper, and chilies and bring to a simmer. Cover and cook over medium-low heat until all of the liquid is absorbed, about 20 minutes.

When the rice is done, fluff the grains and fold in the parsley and scallions. Let stand (still covered) for about 5 minutes before serving.

YIELD: 6 SERVINGS

# Serrano Pilaf

WHOLE SERRANO CHILIES are often simmered in pilafs and then either removed at the finish or served as an edible garnish (but they are still quite hot!).

| | |
|---|---|
| 1 tablespoon canola oil | 2 teaspoons dried oregano |
| 1 medium yellow onion, diced | ½ teaspoon turmeric |
| 1 red bell pepper, seeded and diced | ½ teaspoon black pepper |
| 4 cloves garlic, minced | ½ teaspoon salt |
| 6 to 8 serrano peppers (2 seeded and minced, the rest left whole) | 1½ cups long-grain white rice |
| | 1 cup frozen green peas |
| 1 can (14 ounces) stewed tomatoes, drained | 2 to 3 tablespoons chopped fresh cilantro |

IN A LARGE saucepan, heat the oil. Add the onion, bell pepper, garlic, and minced serrano peppers and cook, stirring, for 5 minutes over medium heat. Stir in the stewed tomatoes, remaining 4 to 6 whole peppers, oregano, turmeric, black pepper, and salt and cook for 1 minute more. Stir in 3 cups water and the rice and bring to a simmer. Stir in the peas, cover, and cook over medium-low heat until all of the liquid is absorbed, about 15 minutes.

Fluff the rice and fold in the cilantro. Let stand for 5 minutes before serving.

YIELD: 6 SERVINGS

# A Flurry of Curry

## GREAT BOWLS OF INDIA

IF MEXICO IS the chili capital of the world, then India must be the spice capital. Venture into an Indian restaurant, and you'll notice the perfume of coriander, cumin, cloves, turmeric, cayenne, and ginger that fills the air. While not every Indian kitchen is a firehouse of spice clanging with incendiary bells and whistles, the cuisine does exude with aromatic seasonings and penetrating flavors. This is not food for the bashful or the meek. Rather, it is for the bold and the adventurous.

**Curry powder** is the marquee flavor of this chapter. The versatile blend of seasoning enlivens everything it embraces—from velvety soups and hearty stews to grain pilafs, pureed legumes, and mixed vegetables. Curry powders range from mild to hot and include a variety of seasonings, including turmeric, cumin, cloves, coriander, black pepper, and cayenne pepper. Depending on the brand or cook, curry powders can also contain cardamom, cinnamon, mustard, and fenugreek.

Curry powder is not subtle; it makes its presence known as soon as it is added to the pot. The secret to cooking with curry is to briefly sear the spices in the hot pan just before adding the liquid. This initial quick searing seems to release the maximum flavor from the dried curry seasonings. The curry will also envelop the entire kitchen with its distinctive fragrance.

Another fragrant spice mixture used in the Indian kitchen is **garam masala** (*masala* generally refers to a blend of aromatic spices). Garam masala typically includes sweet spices, such as cardamom, coriander, cinnamon, cumin, cloves, and nutmeg. Just a touch of garam masala lends a satisfying depth to soups, rice dishes, curries, and stews. It is more string music than percussion and drums.

Great bowls of Indian cuisine include curried chicken; mulligatawny, a gumbo-like soup; sambar, a vegetable and split pea stew; and biryani, a cousin of Spanish paella. Of course, no discourse on Indian cooking would be complete without mention of dal, a luscious dish of lentils or peas, potatoes, and assertive spices. (The name "dal" also refers to specific legumes.)

In addition to a plethora of seasonings, the Indian pantry includes basmati rice, a slender grain with a nutty flavor; pungent cilantro; myriad beans, peas, and lentils (including quick-cooking, pinkish-red lentils); ginger root, cayenne peppers, and garlic; potatoes, carrots, and other vegetables. Soothing yogurt condiments, such as raita and coconut chutney, are often served alongside spicy-hot curry dishes to cool the palate. A wide selection of Indian flat breads (such as nan and roti) are perfect for lapping up the stimulating sauces, soups, dals, and stews.

# Butternut and Red Lentil Soup

RED LENTILS COOK to a thick, porridgelike texture and meld smoothly into this curry-scented squash soup.

1 tablespoon canola oil

1 medium yellow onion, diced

2 carrots, diced

4 cloves garlic, minced

2 teaspoons curry powder

1 teaspoon ground cumin

1 teaspoon garam masala

½ teaspoon cayenne pepper

1 cup red lentils

2 cups peeled, diced butternut squash

¼ cup chopped fresh parsley

1 teaspoon salt

IN A LARGE saucepan, heat the oil. Add the onion, carrots, and garlic and cook, stirring, over medium heat for about 5 minutes. Stir in the curry powder, cumin, garam masala, and cayenne pepper and cook, stirring, for 1 minute over low heat. Add 6 cups water and the lentils and bring to a simmer. Stir in the squash and cook over medium-low heat until the lentils and squash are tender, about 40 minutes, stirring occasionally.

Stir in the parsley and salt and cook for 5 minutes more. Ladle the soup into bowls and serve with warm roti or nan (Indian flat breads).

YIELD: 4 TO 6 SERVINGS

🍴 Shopping Tip

RED LENTILS ARE AVAILABLE IN WELL-STOCKED SUPERMARKETS AND INDIAN GROCERY STORES.

# Gourmet Squash and Lentil Soup

———————————  ✦  ———————————

THIS NOURISHING TUREEN is a squash lover's soup. Baby gourmet squash have a succulent texture and are ideal candidates for flavorful soups and stews.

If you can't find red lentils in your supermarket, the more common green lentils can be used, but they may take 10 to 15 minutes longer to cook.

| | |
|---|---|
| 1 tablespoon canola oil | ½ teaspoon cayenne pepper |
| 1 medium yellow onion, diced | 1 cup red lentils |
| 2 stalks celery, chopped | 2½ cups peeled, diced butternut |
| 4 cloves garlic, minced | squash or red kuri squash |
| 1 fresh cayenne chili pepper, seeded | 8 to 10 baby pattypan squash or |
| and minced | baby zucchini |
| 1 tablespoon curry powder | 2 tablespoons chopped fresh |
| 1 teaspoon ground cumin | cilantro |
| 1 teaspoon garam masala | 1 teaspoon salt |

IN A LARGE saucepan, heat the oil. Add the onion, celery, garlic, and cayenne chili pepper and cook, stirring, for 5 minutes over medium heat. Stir in the curry powder, cumin, garam masala, and cayenne pepper and cook, stirring, for 30 seconds. Stir in 6 cups water and the lentils and bring to a simmer. Cook for 10 minutes over medium heat, stirring occasionally. Stir in the butternut squash and cook for 10 minutes more. Stir in the baby squash and cook until the lentils are tender, about 15 minutes more. Stir in the cilantro and salt and let stand for 5 minutes.

Ladle the soup into bowls and serve at once with traditional Indian bread, such as nan or roti.

YIELD: 6 SERVINGS

### ¶¶¶ Shopping Tip

YOUNG PATTYPAN SQUASH AND RED KURI SQUASH ARE SOLD ON A SEASONAL BASIS AT FARMERS' MARKETS AND AT WELL-STOCKED SUPERMARKETS. RED LENTILS ARE AVAILABLE IN WELL-STOCKED SUPERMARKETS AND INDIAN GROCERY STORES.

### Spice Advice

PLAIN YOGURT OR RAITA MAKES A SOOTHING CONDIMENT.

# Creamy Spinach Masala

THIS DEEP-GREEN BISQUE, imbued with garam masala, is an Indian cousin to Caribbean callaloo soup.

1 tablespoon olive oil

1 medium yellow onion, diced

3 or 4 cloves garlic, minced

8 cups coarsely chopped fresh
spinach

2 cups peeled, diced potatoes

1 large carrot, diced

2 teaspoons garam masala

1 teaspoon ground coriander

½ teaspoon cayenne pepper

½ teaspoon salt

1 cup whole milk

IN A LARGE saucepan, heat the oil. Add the onion and garlic and cook, stirring, for 4 minutes over medium heat. Add the spinach and cook, stirring, until the leaves are wilted, about 2 minutes. Add 3 cups water, the potatoes, carrot, garam masala, coriander, cayenne pepper, and salt and bring to a simmer. Cook over medium heat until the potatoes are tender, about 20 minutes, stirring occasionally.

Transfer the soup to a blender or a food processor fitted with a steel blade and process until smooth, about 10 seconds.

Return the soup to the pan and stir in the milk. Set the pan over medium heat and bring the soup to a gentle simmer, stirring frequently.

Ladle the bisque into bowls and serve at once. Offer warm Indian flat bread or pita bread.

YIELD: 4 SERVINGS

🍴 *Shopping Tip*

ONE 10-OUNCE BAG OF SPINACH
WILL YIELD 8 TO 10 CUPS OF
CHOPPED SPINACH.

*Some Like It Hotter*

ADD 2 SERRANO OR JALAPEÑO
PEPPERS (SEEDED AND MINCED)
TO THE PAN ALONG WITH
THE ONION AND GARLIC.

# Bombay Chicken Mulligatawny

THERE ARE MANY varieties of mulligatawny soup, and all are boldly seasoned with aromatic spices. This fragrant hot pot is no exception.

½ cup green lentils, rinsed

1 tablespoon canola oil

¾ pound boneless chicken breasts or thighs, diced

1 medium yellow onion, diced

1 large tomato, diced

4 cloves garlic, minced

1 tablespoon minced ginger root

1 tablespoon curry powder

1½ teaspoons ground cumin

1 teaspoon garam masala

½ teaspoon cayenne pepper

2 carrots, diced

1 large potato, diced

2 to 3 tablespoons chopped fresh cilantro

1 teaspoon salt

4 cups cooked basmati or long-grain white rice

IN A LARGE saucepan, combine the lentils with 7 cups water and bring to a simmer over medium-high heat. Cook over medium-low heat until tender (but not mushy), about 25 minutes, stirring occasionally. Remove from the heat and set aside.

In another large saucepan heat the oil. Add the chicken, onion, tomato, garlic, and ginger and cook, stirring, for 7 minutes over medium heat. Add the curry powder, cumin, garam masala, and cayenne pepper and cook, stirring, for 1 minute more. Add the lentils with their cooking liquid, carrots, and potato and bring to a simmer. Cook over medium-low heat until the potato is tender, about 20 minutes, stirring occasionally. Stir in the cilantro and salt.

To serve, spoon the rice into bowls and ladle the mulligatawny over the top. Serve with Indian flat bread or pita bread.

YIELD: 6 SERVINGS

### Some Like It Hotter

GENEROUSLY ADD
BOTTLED RED HOT SAUCE
TO THE FINISHED SOUP.

# Vegetable Mulligatawny

MULLIGATAWNY, WHICH MEANS "pepper water," is an Indian cousin of Cajun gumbo.

1 tablespoon canola oil

1 medium yellow onion, diced

4 cloves garlic, minced

1 tablespoon minced ginger
    root

1 large tomato, diced

2 teaspoons curry powder

1½ teaspoons ground cumin

½ teaspoon ground coriander

½ teaspoon cayenne pepper

¾ cup red lentils

2 carrots, diced

1 large potato, diced

2½ cups coarsely chopped spinach
    or kale

1 teaspoon salt

4 cups cooked basmati or long-grain
    white rice

IN A LARGE saucepan, heat the oil. Add the onion, garlic, and ginger and cook, stirring, for 4 minutes over medium heat. Add the tomato, curry powder, cumin, coriander, and cayenne pepper and cook, stirring, for 1 minute more. Add 6 cups water, the lentils, carrots, and potato and bring to a simmer. Cook over medium-low heat until the lentils are tender, about 35 minutes, stirring occasionally. Stir in the spinach and salt and cook for 5 to 10 minutes more.

Spoon the rice into bowls and ladle the mulligatawny over the top. Serve with Indian flat bread or pita bread.

YIELD: 6 SERVINGS

### Shopping Tip

LOOK FOR RED LENTILS AND BASMATI RICE IN NATURAL FOOD STORES, WELL-STOCKED SUPERMARKETS, OR INDIAN GROCERY STORES.

# Curried Chicken with Sweet Potatoes

CURRY SEASONINGS AND chicken go hand in hand. The mild, humdrum nature of poultry benefits from a contingent of assertive spices and cayenne peppers.

1 tablespoon canola oil

1 medium yellow onion, diced

1 medium tomato, diced

4 cloves garlic, minced

1 or 2 fresh cayenne chili peppers,
    seeded and minced

1 tablespoon minced ginger root

1 tablespoon curry powder

1 teaspoon ground cumin

½ teaspoon turmeric

½ teaspoon salt

1 pound boneless chicken thighs or
    breasts, diced

2 carrots, diced

1 large sweet potato, diced

1½ cups chicken broth or water

IN A MEDIUM saucepan, heat the oil. Add the onion, tomato, garlic, cayenne chili pepper, and ginger and cook, stirring, for 5 minutes over medium-high heat. Add the curry powder, cumin, turmeric, and salt and cook, stirring, for 1 minute more. Add the chicken and cook, stirring, for 5 or 6 minutes more.

Add the carrots, sweet potato, and broth and bring to a simmer. Cook for 20 to 25 minutes over medium heat, stirring occasionally, until the vegetables are tender and the chicken is fully cooked. Remove from the heat and let stand for about 5 minutes before serving.

Ladle the curry into bowls and serve with basmati rice on the side.

YIELD: 3 OR 4 SERVINGS

# Seafood and Chicken Biryani

BIRYANI IS A spicy Indian version of paella. This version is revved up with serrano chilies and cayenne pepper.

| | |
|---|---|
| 1 tablespoon canola oil | 2 medium tomatoes, diced |
| 1 medium yellow onion, diced | 1 tablespoon curry powder |
| 1 red bell pepper, seeded and diced | 1 teaspoon salt |
| 4 cloves garlic, minced | ½ teaspoon ground fenugreek or ginger |
| 2 serrano peppers, seeded and minced | ½ teaspoon cayenne pepper |
| 1 pound boneless chicken thighs, diced | ½ teaspoon turmeric |
| ½ to ¾ pound medium shrimp, peeled and deveined | 3 cups water or chicken broth |
| | 1½ cups basmati rice |
| | 1 cup green peas, fresh or frozen |

IN A LARGE saucepan, heat the oil. Add the onion, bell pepper, garlic, and serrano peppers and cook, stirring, for 5 minutes over medium heat. Add the chicken and cook, stirring, for 4 minutes. Add the shrimp, tomatoes, curry powder, salt, fenugreek, cayenne pepper, and turmeric and cook, stirring, for 4 minutes more. Stir in the water and rice and bring to a simmer. Stir in the peas, cover the pan, and cook over medium-low heat until all of the liquid is absorbed, about 15 to 20 minutes.

Fluff the grains and let stand for 5 to 10 minutes before serving. Ladle into bowls and serve with nan or roti bread.

YIELD: 4 SERVINGS

# Curried Spinach and Potatoes

THIS SPICY VEGETABLE stew can be served as a side dish or piled over rice and served as a main dish.

| | |
|---|---|
| 1 tablespoon canola oil | 1 teaspoon garam masala |
| 1 medium yellow onion, diced | ½ teaspoon salt |
| 2 cloves garlic, minced | ½ teaspoon cayenne pepper |
| 2 jalapeño or serrano peppers, seeded and minced | ¼ teaspoon turmeric |
| | 4 cups water or vegetable broth |
| 1 can (14 ounces) stewed tomatoes | 2 cups diced potatoes |
| | 2 carrots, diced |
| 1 tablespoon curry powder | 1 package (10 ounces) frozen chopped spinach, thawed |
| 1 teaspoon ground cumin | |

IN A LARGE saucepan, heat the oil. Add the onion, garlic, and chili peppers and cook, stirring, for 4 minutes over medium heat. Add the tomatoes, curry powder, cumin, garam masala, salt, cayenne pepper, and turmeric and cook, stirring, for 3 minutes more. Add the water, potatoes, and carrots and bring to a simmer. Cook over medium heat for 20 minutes, stirring occasionally.

Stir in the spinach and cook for about 10 minutes over medium-low heat, stirring occasionally. To thicken, mash some of the potatoes against the side of the pan with the back of a spoon. Let stand for 5 minutes before serving.

Ladle into bowls and serve with warm Indian flat bread.

YIELD: 6 SERVINGS

# Sri Lankan Split Pea Sambar

SAMBAR IS A thick stew of curried vegetables, potatoes, and split peas or lentils. It is almost always accompanied by basmati rice and coconut chutney or raita.

To accelerate the cooking process, soak the split peas for 30 minutes to 1 hour ahead of time.

| | |
|---|---|
| ½ cup yellow split peas | 1 teaspoon ground coriander |
| 1 tablespoon canola oil | 1 teaspoon ground ginger |
| 1 medium yellow onion, diced | 1 teaspoon salt |
| 2 carrots, diced | ½ teaspoon cayenne pepper |
| 3 or 4 cloves garlic, minced | ¼ teaspoon turmeric |
| 1 large tomato, diced | 1 large potato, diced |
| 1 tablespoon curry powder | 10 or 12 broccoli florets |

IN A LARGE saucepan, combine the split peas and 5 cups water and bring to a simmer. Cook for about 45 minutes over medium heat, stirring occasionally. Set aside.

In another large saucepan, heat the oil. Add the onion, carrots, and garlic and cook, stirring, for 5 minutes over medium heat. Stir in the tomato, curry powder, coriander, ginger, salt, cayenne pepper, and turmeric and cook, stirring, for 1 minute more. Add the split peas with their cooking liquid and the potato and bring to a simmer. Cook for 20 to 25 minutes over medium heat until the potatoes are tender, stirring occasionally. Add the broccoli and cook, stirring, for 5 minutes more. Let stand 5 to 10 minutes before serving.

Ladle the sambar into bowls and serve with traditional Indian accompaniments.

YIELD: 4 SERVINGS

### Some Like It Hotter

ADD 2 SERRANO CHILIES (MINCED) WITH THE SAUTÉED VEGETABLES.

# Curried Squash in a Bowl

———————— 🌶 ————————

PUNGENT CURRY SEASONINGS enliven the quiet flavors of winter squash. You can serve the curried squash as a spicy side dish or light main dish. If butternut squash is unavailable, substitute with buttercup or Hubbard squash.

| | |
|---|---|
| 1 tablespoon canola oil | 1 teaspoon ground coriander |
| 2 medium tomatoes, diced | ½ teaspoon cayenne pepper |
| 1 medium yellow onion, diced | ½ teaspoon turmeric |
| 3 or 4 cloves garlic, minced | ½ teaspoon salt |
| 2 red Fresno or fresh cayenne | 2½ cups peeled, diced butternut squash |
|    chili peppers, seeded and minced | 1 cup cooked or canned (drained) |
| 1 tablespoon minced ginger root |    chick-peas |
| 1 tablespoon curry powder | 3 to 4 cups cooked basmati rice |

IN A MEDIUM saucepan, heat the oil. Add the tomatoes, onion, garlic, chili peppers, and ginger and cook, stirring, for 4 minutes over medium-high heat. Add the curry powder, coriander, cayenne pepper, turmeric, and salt and cook, stirring, for 1 minute more. Stir in the squash and 1½ cups water and bring to a simmer. Cook over medium heat until the squash is tender, about 25 minutes. Stir in the chick-peas and cook for 3 to 4 minutes more.

Spoon the rice into bowls and ladle the curried squash over the top.

YIELD: 4 SERVINGS

✗ Spice Advice

PLAIN YOGURT IS A COOLING
CONDIMENT TO SPOON OVER THE CURRY.

# Aloo Beingan (Eggplant and Potato Curry)

EGGPLANT AND POTATOES form a tasty alliance in this traditional meatless stew.

| | |
|---|---|
| 1½ tablespoons canola oil | 1 tablespoon curry powder |
| 1 medium yellow onion, diced | 1 tablespoon dried parsley |
| 1 green bell pepper, seeded and diced | 1 teaspoon garam masala |
| 2½ cups diced eggplant | 1 teaspoon salt |
| 2 medium tomatoes, diced | ½ teaspoon black pepper |
| 3 or 4 cloves garlic, minced | 2 cups diced potatoes |
| 1 fresh cayenne or serrano pepper, seeded and minced | 1 cup cooked or canned (drained) chick-peas |

IN A MEDIUM saucepan, heat the oil. Add the onion, bell pepper, and eggplant and cook, stirring, for 7 minutes over medium heat. Add the tomatoes, garlic, and chili pepper and cook, stirring, for 4 minutes more. Add the curry powder, parsley, garam masala, salt, and black pepper and cook, stirring, for 1 minute more.

Add the potatoes and 2 cups water and bring to a simmer. Cook for 20 to 25 minutes over medium heat, stirring occasionally, until the potatoes are tender. Stir in the chick-peas and cook for 5 minutes more.

Serve the curried stew over a bowl of basmati rice.

YIELD: 4 SERVINGS

Spice Advice

OFFER PLAIN YOGURT AS A SOOTHING CONDIMENT.

# Curried Chick-Peas with Potatoes

THIS TASTY DAL is prepared with nutty chick-peas. Although chick-peas take a while to cook from scratch, the savory result is well worth the wait. Remember, dried chick-peas should be soaked in plenty of water for several hours before cooking; after draining, cook the legumes in fresh water. Serve this as a side dish or appetizer.

1 cup dried chick-peas, soaked
    overnight and drained

1 tablespoon canola oil

1 medium yellow onion, finely chopped

2 cloves garlic, minced

2 teaspoons minced ginger root

2 serrano or jalapeño peppers, seeded
    and minced

1 medium tomato, diced

1 tablespoon curry powder

1 teaspoon ground cumin

¼ teaspoon turmeric

¼ teaspoon cayenne pepper

2 cups peeled, diced
    potatoes

1 teaspoon salt

IN A MEDIUM saucepan, combine the chick-peas and 6 cups water and bring to a simmer. Cook over medium-low heat until the chick-peas are tender, 1 to 1½ hours. Drain the chick-peas, reserving 2 cups of the cooking liquid.

In a medium saucepan, heat the oil. Add the onion, garlic, ginger, and chili peppers and cook, stirring, for 4 minutes over medium heat. Add the tomato, curry powder, cumin, turmeric, and cayenne pepper and cook, stirring, 3 minutes more. Stir in the chick-peas, cooking liquid, and potatoes and bring to a simmer. Cook over medium heat for 25 to 30 minutes, stirring occasionally, until the potatoes are tender. Stir in the salt. With the back of a large spoon, mash the chick-peas and potatoes as you stir.

Transfer the dal to a serving bowl. Serve warm Indian flat bread (such as roti or nan) to dip into the dal.

YIELD: 6 SERVINGS

### Some Like It Hotter

ADD ½ TEASPOON BLACK PEPPER AND ½ TEASPOON WHITE PEPPER ALONG WITH THE OTHER SEASONINGS.

# Sweet Potato Dal

WHEN MAKING THIS dish of lentils and sweet potatoes, patience is a virtue. You must slow-cook the legumes until a smooth, pureed consistency is reached. A good well-cooked dal will melt in your mouth. Do not rush it; dal is not fast food. Serve as a side dish or appetizer.

1 tablespoon canola oil

1 medium yellow onion, finely
   chopped

4 cloves garlic, minced

1 or 2 serrano or jalapeño peppers,
   seeded and minced

2 teaspoons curry powder

½ teaspoon ground cumin

½ teaspoon ground coriander or
   garam masala

½ teaspoon cayenne pepper

¼ teaspoon turmeric

1 cup green lentils, rinsed

2 cups peeled, diced sweet
   potatoes

1 teaspoon salt

IN A MEDIUM saucepan, heat the oil. Add the onion, garlic, and chili pepper and cook, stirring, for 4 minutes over medium-high heat. Stir in the curry powder, cumin, coriander, cayenne pepper, and turmeric and cook for 30 seconds more. Stir in the lentils and 4½ cups water and bring to a simmer. Cook over medium heat for 15 minutes, stirring occasionally. Stir in the sweet potatoes and cook for 25 to 30 minutes more, stirring occasionally, until the lentils are tender. Stir in the salt.

Transfer the dal to a large serving bowl. Serve with warm Indian flat breads or flour tortillas.

YIELD: 4 SERVINGS

# CHAPTER SEVEN

# Soul in a Bowl

## HOT POTS OF AFRICA

AFRICA HAS MADE lasting contributions to the world's cuisine. From West Africa came jollof rice, a festive one-pot party dish and forerunner to Creole jambalaya. The gumbos prepared in Cajun and Caribbean kitchens have roots in African okra stews ("gumbo" comes from the African word for okra). Collard greens, black-eyed peas, corn bread, and plantains—favorite foods of the Deep South—also can be traced to African beginnings.

West African cooking features meat and vegetable stews made with native groundnuts—otherwise known as peanuts. (By the way, peanuts are neither peas nor nuts; they are legumes.) Groundnuts are cooked and pureed into thick, nutty concoctions and seasoned with ginger, garlic, tomatoes, and earthy spices. Another favorite is Chicken Yassa, a mountainous lemony stew served over a pile of rice or couscous. Doro wat is an aromatic Ethiopian stew with spicy underpinnings.

The North African cuisine practiced in Morocco and Tunisia offers hearty stews called tagines—one-pot creations made with meat or chicken, sturdy vegetables, dried fruits, and aromatic seasonings. Tagines are often served with couscous, the North African grainlike pasta. The key spice of the region is called **harissa,** a wet, brick-red chili paste with a rustic quality and pervasive flavor. Although harissa is hard to find, it is worth the extra effort.

# Jollof Chicken Rice

THIS ANCESTOR OF jambalaya is served at parties and festive celebrations throughout West Africa. It can be made with seafood, meat, or vegetables.

1 tablespoon canola oil

¾ pound boneless chicken breasts or
    thighs, diced

1 medium yellow onion, diced

1 green bell pepper, seeded and diced

1 tablespoon minced ginger root

2 medium tomatoes, diced

2 teaspoons curry powder

2 teaspoons dried thyme

½ teaspoon cayenne pepper

½ teaspoon salt

1½ cups long-grain white rice

2 carrots, diced

1 tablespoon tomato paste

2 cups chopped leafy greens (such as
    collards or spinach)

IN A LARGE saucepan, heat the oil. Add the chicken and cook, stirring, over medium-high heat until browned, about 5 minutes. Stir in the onion, bell pepper, and ginger and cook, stirring, for 6 minutes more. Add the tomatoes, curry powder, thyme, cayenne pepper, and salt and cook over medium heat, stirring, for 3 minutes more. Stir in the rice, 3 cups water, the carrots, tomato paste, and greens and bring to a simmer. Stir the grains, cover the pan, and cook over medium-low heat until all of the liquid is absorbed, about 20 minutes.

Fluff the grains and let stand for 10 minutes before serving. Spoon into bowls and serve at once.

YIELD: 4 SERVINGS

# Ethiopian Chicken Stew

INSPIRED BY AN Ethiopian dish called doro wat, this is an aromatic, spicy, and intensely flavored chicken stew. Serve it with injera, an elastic Ethiopian bread perfect for scooping and dipping.

1 tablespoon canola oil

1 large yellow onion, diced

4 cloves garlic, minced

1 tablespoon minced ginger root

1 or 2 fresh cayenne or serrano peppers, seeded and minced

1 pound boneless chicken thighs or breasts, diced

1 tablespoon paprika

1 teaspoon ground cumin

1 teaspoon ground coriander

1 teaspoon red pepper flakes

1 teaspoon salt

½ teaspoon black pepper

¼ teaspoon ground cinnamon or nutmeg

2 cups chicken broth or water

2 cups diced potatoes

2 carrots, diced

¼ cup dry red wine

2 tablespoons tomato paste

Juice of 1 lemon

IN A LARGE saucepan, heat the oil. Add the onion, garlic, ginger, and chili pepper and cook, stirring, for 4 minutes over medium-high heat. Add the chicken and cook, stirring, for 4 minutes more. Add the paprika, cumin, coriander, red pepper flakes, salt, black pepper, and cinnamon and cook, stirring, for 2 minutes over medium-low heat. Add the broth, potatoes, carrots, and wine and bring to a simmer. Cook for 15 minutes over medium heat, stirring occasionally.

Stir in the tomato paste and lemon juice and cook until the potatoes are tender and the chicken is fully cooked, about 5 to 10 minutes.

Serve the stew in wide bowls. Couscous or rice makes a fine bed for the stew.

YIELD: 4 SERVINGS

### Some Like It Hotter

ADD ½ TEASPOON GROUND CAYENNE PEPPER AND A FEW TEASPOONS OF BOTTLED RED HOT SAUCE.

# West African Groundnut Stew

---

SWEET POTATOES, TOMATOES, and peanuts form the foundation of this rich, nutty vegetable stew.

1 tablespoon canola oil

1 medium yellow onion, diced

1 yellow or red bell pepper, seeded
   and diced

2 large cloves garlic, minced

2 teaspoons minced ginger root

1 or 2 fresh cayenne or serrano
   peppers, seeded and minced

2 cups tomato juice

1 can (14 ounces) stewed tomatoes

1 medium sweet potato, diced

1½ teaspoons dried thyme

1½ teaspoons ground cumin

½ teaspoon black pepper

½ teaspoon salt

2 cups shredded green chard or
   spinach

½ to ¾ cup chunky peanut butter

IN A LARGE saucepan, heat the oil. Add the onion, bell pepper, garlic, ginger, and chili pepper and cook, stirring, for 5 minutes over medium heat. Stir in 2 cups water, the tomato juice, stewed tomatoes, sweet potato, thyme, cumin, black pepper, and salt and bring to a simmer. Cook for 20 to 25 minutes over medium-low heat until the potatoes are tender, stirring occasionally.

Stir in the chard and peanut butter and return to a gentle simmer, stirring frequently. Remove from the heat and let stand for 5 minutes before serving.

Ladle into bowls and serve with a side of couscous or rice.

YIELD: 6 SERVINGS

# Chicken Yassa

HAILING FROM SENEGAL, this is a lemon-flavored stew with strong onion and herbal overtones.

1 pound boneless chicken thighs or
    breasts, diced

Juice of 2 large lemons

1 tablespoon canola oil

2 medium yellow onions, slivered

4 cloves garlic, minced

1 or 2 fresh cayenne or serrano
    peppers, seeded and minced

2 cups chicken broth or water

2 cups diced potatoes

2 carrots, diced

¼ cup dry white wine

1 tablespoon dried parsley

1 teaspoon salt

½ teaspoon dried thyme

½ teaspoon black pepper

1½ cups boiling water

1 cup couscous

COMBINE THE CHICKEN and lemon juice in a mixing bowl. Cover and refrigerate for 30 minutes to 1 hour.

In a large saucepan, heat the oil. Add the onions, garlic, and chili pepper and cook, stirring, for 5 minutes over medium-high heat. Stir in the chicken and cook, stirring, for 4 minutes. Add the broth, potatoes, carrots, wine, parsley, salt, thyme, and black pepper and bring to a simmer. Cook for 20 minutes over medium heat, stirring occasionally, until the potatoes are tender and the chicken is fully cooked.

Meanwhile, combine the boiling water and couscous in a bowl, and cover. Let stand for 10 minutes. Fluff the grains, cover the pot, and let stand until the stew is ready. Spoon the couscous into bowls and ladle the chicken stew over the top.

YIELD: 4 SERVINGS

# Moroccan Harissa Beef Stew

HARISSA IS THE pungent spice paste prevalent in North African cooking. It is a husky blend of cumin, coriander, pepper, and garlic, which complements the robust nature of beef.

1 tablespoon canola oil

1 medium yellow onion, diced

1 red bell pepper, seeded and diced

2 cloves garlic, minced

1 pound sirloin tip or top round, cubed

1 can (14 ounces) stewed tomatoes, drained

2 tablespoons harissa

½ teaspoon cayenne pepper

½ teaspoon salt

2 cups chicken broth or water

2 cups peeled, diced butternut squash or sweet potatoes

1 can (15 ounces) chick-peas, drained

¼ cup chopped fresh parsley

2¼ cups boiling water

1½ cups couscous

IN A LARGE saucepan, heat the oil. Add the onion, bell pepper, and garlic and cook, stirring, for 4 minutes over medium-high heat. Add the beef and cook, stirring, until browned, about 5 minutes. Add the tomatoes, harissa, cayenne pepper, and salt and cook over medium heat, stirring, for 2 minutes more. Add the broth and squash and bring to a simmer. Cook for 15 minutes over medium heat, stirring occasionally. Stir in the chick-peas and parsley and cook, stirring, for 5 to 10 minutes more, until the squash is tender.

Meanwhile, combine the boiling water and couscous in a bowl and cover. Let stand for 10 minutes. Fluff the grains and let stand (still covered) until the stew is ready.

Spoon the couscous into wide bowls and ladle the stew over the top. Serve at once.

YIELD: 4 SERVINGS

### ♉ Shopping Tip

HARISSA IS AVAILABLE IN THE SPECIALTY SECTION OF WELL-STOCKED SUPERMARKETS.

### ☙ Some Like It Hotter

ADD 1 OR 2 FRESH CAYENNE PEPPERS (SEEDED AND MINCED) TO THE PAN ALONG WITH THE BEEF.

# Chicken and Pumpkin Tagine

TAGINES ARE STEWS made with meats, vegetables, dried fruits, and sweet spices. At first, the idea of raisins and cinnamon in a stew did not excite me, but once I tasted this savory tagine, I was converted.

1 tablespoon canola oil

1 medium yellow onion, diced

3 or 4 cloves garlic, minced

1 pound boneless chicken thighs, diced

1 to 2 tablespoons harissa

1 teaspoon ground cumin

1 teaspoon ground coriander

½ teaspoon salt

¼ teaspoon ground cinnamon

2 cups chicken broth

2 cups peeled, diced fresh pumpkin or
   butternut squash

1 large potato, diced

⅓ cup raisins

1 cup cooked or canned (drained)
   fava beans or chick-peas

2¼ cups boiling water

1½ cups couscous

IN A LARGE saucepan, heat the oil. Add the onion and garlic and cook, stirring, for 4 minutes over medium-high heat. Add the chicken and cook, stirring, until browned, about 5 minutes. Add the harissa, cumin, coriander, salt, and cinnamon and cook over medium-low heat, stirring, for 1 minute more. Add the broth, pumpkin, potato, and raisins and bring to a simmer. Cook for 20 minutes over medium-low heat, stirring occasionally. Add the beans and cook for 5 minutes more.

Meanwhile, combine the boiling water and couscous in a medium bowl and cover. Let stand for 10 minutes. Fluff the grains and let stand (covered) until the stew is ready.

Spoon the couscous into wide bowls and ladle the stew over the top. Serve at once.

YIELD: 4 SERVINGS

🍴 *Shopping Tip*

HARISSA IS SOLD IN THE SPECIALTY SECTION OF WELL-STOCKED SUPERMARKETS. TAGINES ARE TRADITIONALLY SEASONED WITH AN EXOTIC (AND HARD TO FIND) SPICE MIXTURE CALLED RAS EL HANOUT. IF YOU FIND IT, ADD A TEASPOON TO THE STEW ALONG WITH THE HARISSA.

🐛 *Some Like It Hot*

ADD ½ TEASPOON GROUND CAYENNE PEPPER ALONG WITH THE OTHER SEASONINGS.

# Eggplant and Fava Bean Tagine

THIS RATATOUILLE-LIKE STEW is a cauldron of earthy fava beans, tomatoes, and chewy eggplant. Couscous soaks up the flavors.

2 tablespoons canola oil

1 medium yellow onion, diced

1 red bell pepper, seeded and diced

3 or 4 cloves garlic, minced

2 cups diced eggplant

1 can (14 ounces) stewed tomatoes

1 can (14 ounces) crushed
 tomatoes

1½ cups cooked or canned (drained)
 fava beans or chick-peas

2 tablespoons harissa

1 teaspoon ground cumin

1 teaspoon ground ginger

½ teaspoon salt

2¼ cups boiling water

1½ cups couscous

IN A LARGE saucepan, heat the oil. Add the onion, bell pepper, garlic, and eggplant and cook, stirring, for 8 to 10 minutes over medium heat. Add the stewed tomatoes, crushed tomatoes, beans, harissa, cumin, ginger, and salt and bring to a simmer. Cook for 15 to 20 minutes over medium-low heat, stirring occasionally.

Meanwhile, combine the boiling water and couscous in a medium bowl and cover. Let stand for 10 minutes. Fluff the grains and let stand (covered) until the stew is ready. Spoon the couscous into wide bowls and ladle the stew over the top.

YIELD: 4 SERVINGS

*Shopping Tip*

HARISSA IS SOLD IN THE SPECIALTY SECTION
OF WELL-STOCKED SUPERMARKETS.

# Spicy Groundnut Chicken

———————————

THIS LUSCIOUS CHICKEN and peanut stew elevates the role of peanut butter to epicurean status.

1 tablespoon canola oil

1 medium yellow onion, diced

1 green bell pepper, seeded and diced

2 medium tomatoes, diced

2 large cloves garlic, minced

1 tablespoon minced ginger root

1 or 2 fresh cayenne or serrano peppers, seeded and minced

1 pound boneless chicken thighs, diced

½ cup water or chicken broth

½ cup tomato juice

1 teaspoon ground cumin

½ teaspoon dried thyme

½ teaspoon cayenne pepper

½ teaspoon salt

½ to ¾ cup chunky peanut butter

4 cups cooked long-grain white rice, basmati rice, or couscous

IN A LARGE saucepan, heat the oil. Add the onion, bell pepper, tomatoes, garlic, ginger, and chili pepper and cook, stirring, for 4 minutes over medium heat. Stir in the chicken and cook, stirring, for 10 minutes more. Stir in the water, tomato juice, cumin, thyme, cayenne pepper, and salt and bring to a simmer. Cook for 10 to 15 minutes over medium heat until the chicken is cooked in the center, stirring occasionally.

Stir in the peanut butter and cook for about 5 minutes over low heat, stirring frequently. Spoon the rice or couscous into bowls and ladle the stew over the top.

YIELD: 4 SERVINGS

# Gumbo Ya Ya

THIS FORERUNNER TO Louisiana gumbo is brimming with okra, chicken, greens, and herbs.

1 tablespoon canola oil

1 medium yellow onion, diced

1 green bell pepper, seeded and diced

4 cloves garlic, minced

¾ pound boneless chicken breasts or thighs, diced

4 cups chicken broth

1 can (14 ounces) stewed tomatoes

8 to 10 collard leaves, cut into strips

1 cup fresh or frozen chopped okra

2 teaspoons dried oregano

1 teaspoon dried thyme

½ teaspoon black pepper

½ teaspoon salt

½ teaspoon cayenne pepper

½ cup tomato paste

4 cups cooked long-grain white rice

IN A LARGE saucepan, heat the oil. Add the onion, bell pepper, and garlic and cook, stirring, for 6 minutes over medium-high heat. Add the chicken and cook, stirring, for 3 to 4 minutes more. Add the broth, stewed tomatoes, collard strips, okra, oregano, thyme, black pepper, salt, and cayenne pepper and bring to a simmer. Cook over medium heat for 15 minutes, stirring occasionally. Stir in the tomato paste and cook for 10 minutes more.

Spoon the rice into shallow bowls and ladle the gumbo over the top. Serve with warm corn bread.

YIELD: 6 SERVINGS

### Some Like It Hotter

SEASON THE GUMBO WITH BOTTLED RED HOT SAUCE AND RED PEPPER FLAKES.

# CHAPTER EIGHT

# Prize Bowls of the Pacific Rim

PACIFIC RIM CUISINE offers a culinary ballet of tastes, textures, and pleasures. There are a pantheon of bowls beckoning with enticement, from Thai Curry Scallops with Basil and Szechuan Noodle Soup to Evil Jungle Peanut Chicken and Chicken Firepot with Shiitake Mushrooms. Pacific flavors strike a harmonious balance between hot and fragrant, mellow and sharp, and tender and crisp. A yin-and-yang philosophy pervades the kitchen.

In the simmering soups, firepots, and one-pot dishes, Asian hot peppers share the stage with indispensable condiments and pastes. The ubiquitous **chili-garlic paste** is a thick, brick-red sauce that can fire up a bowl in seconds. A variety of **Thai curry pastes**—potent concoctions of chilies, garlic, and pungent spices—combined with rich coconut milk are the foundation of Thai curry sauces and soups. **Szechuan paste,** made from Szechuan peppercorns, exudes with a floral pungency and radiates true meltdown potential. **Sambals** from Indonesia are glistening sweet-and-hot chili pastes guaranteed to slay your taste buds. Taken together, these dynamic condiments are the pillars of spicy Pan-Asian cuisine.

In addition to an array of hot condiments and pastes, fresh and dried chilies such as **Thai bird peppers, chile de arbols,** and **cayenne peppers** are used throughout the region. The Pacific Rim pantry also includes soy sauce, rice vinegar, limes, peanut butter, coconut milk, and plenty of rice and noodles to soak up the rivers of flavor. Fish sauce—a salty, fermented sauce—is prevalent throughout Southeast Asia. Indonesian cuisine offers ketjap manis, a sweetened syrupy version of soy sauce (it can be addicting). Fresh herbs such as anise-scented Thai basil, palate-cleansing cilantro, and citrusy lemon grass provide herbal synergy to the pots.

# Szechuan Noodle Soup

SZECHUAN SAUCE IS an oozing red paste made with Szechuan peppers. It imbues this brothy Asian vegetable soup with rustic, pungent flavor.

10 to 12 ounces lo mein noodles

1 tablespoon peanut oil

1 red bell pepper, seeded and cut into thin strips

8 ounces mushrooms, halved

2 carrots, thinly sliced at an angle

2 cloves garlic, minced

3 cups sliced bok choy leaves

4 cups vegetable broth or chicken broth

¼ pound extra-firm tofu, diced

3 tablespoons soy sauce (preferably low sodium)

1 tablespoon sesame oil

3 to 4 teaspoons Szechuan sauce

2 tablespoons peanut butter

IN A LARGE saucepan, bring 3 quarts of water to a boil over medium-high heat. Place the noodles in the boiling water, stir, and return to a boil. Cook until al dente, 4 to 5 minutes, stirring occasionally. Drain the noodles in a colander.

Meanwhile, in another large saucepan, heat the oil. Add the bell pepper, mushrooms, carrots, and garlic and cook, stirring, for 7 minutes over medium-high heat. Stir in the bok choy and cook, stirring, for 3 to 4 minutes more. Stir in the broth, tofu, soy sauce, sesame oil, and Szechuan sauce and bring to a simmer. Cook for about 10 minutes over medium heat, stirring occasionally. Reduce the heat to low and blend in the peanut butter.

Using tongs, place the noodles in large bowls. Ladle the brothy vegetables over the top and serve at once.

YIELD: 6 SERVINGS

# Javanese Chicken Soup

THIS INDONESIAN VERSION of chicken noodle soup is flavored with lime, coconut, peanut butter, ginger, and chili-garlic paste.

2 tablespoons peanut oil

½ pound boneless chicken breasts or
    thighs, diced

1 medium yellow onion, diced

2 large cloves garlic, minced

1 tablespoon minced ginger
    root

4 cups chicken broth

1 cup snow peas, halved

1 teaspoon ground cumin

1 teaspoon ground coriander

¼ cup canned coconut milk

¼ cup chunky peanut butter

¼ cup soy sauce (preferably
    low sodium) or ketjap manis

Juice of 2 limes

1 to 2 teaspoons chili-garlic paste or
    sambal

2 whole scallions, chopped

1¾ ounces cellophane noodles

IN A LARGE skillet, heat 1 tablespoon of the oil over medium-high heat. Add the chicken and cook, stirring, until slightly browned and fully cooked, about 7 minutes. Set aside.

In a medium saucepan, heat the remaining 1 tablespoon oil over medium heat. Add the onion, garlic, and ginger and cook, stirring, for 3 minutes. Add the chicken broth, snow peas, cumin, coriander, and cooked chicken and bring to a simmer. Cook for 10 minutes over medium heat, stirring occasionally. Stir in the coconut milk, peanut butter, soy sauce, lime juice, chili-garlic paste, and scallions and bring to a gentle simmer.

Stir the noodles into the soup and continue cooking over medium heat for 5 minutes.

Ladle the soup into bowls and serve at once.

YIELD: 6 SERVINGS

### Shopping Tip

KETJAP MANIS IS AVAILABLE IN ASIAN GROCERY STORES AND WELL-STOCKED SUPERMARKETS.

### Some Like It Hotter

ADD 2 SERRANO PEPPERS (SEEDED AND MINCED) TO THE PAN ALONG WITH THE GARLIC AND GINGER.

# Ramen-Style Noodles and Shiitake-Ginger Soup

RAMEN NOODLES, ALSO called chuka soba or curly Japanese noodles, soak up this marvelously piquant mushroomy broth.

1 package (5 ounces) chuka soba
   noodles
1 tablespoon peanut oil
¼ pound fresh shiitake mushrooms,
   sliced
2 carrots, thinly sliced at an angle
1 red bell pepper, seeded and cut into
   thin strips
1 tablespoon minced ginger root
2 cups sliced bok choy leaves

4 cups vegetable broth
1 can (8 ounces) sliced water chestnuts, drained
¼ pound extra-firm tofu, diced
   (optional)
3 tablespoons soy sauce (preferably
   low sodium)
2 teaspoons sesame oil
3 to 4 teaspoons Szechuan sauce
1½ tablespoons cornstarch

IN A LARGE saucepan, bring 3 quarts of water to a boil over medium-high heat. Place the noodles in the boiling water. When the noodles rise to the top, gently stir and cook until al dente, about 4 to 5 minutes. Drain the noodles in a colander and briefly rinse under running water.

Meanwhile, in another large saucepan, heat the oil. Add the mushrooms, carrots, bell pepper, and ginger and cook, stirring, for 7 minutes over medium heat. Stir in the bok choy and cook, stirring, for 3 minutes more. Stir in the broth, water chestnuts, optional tofu, soy sauce, sesame oil, and Szechuan sauce and bring to a simmer. Cook for about 10 minutes over medium heat, stirring occasionally.

In a small mixing bowl, whisk together the cornstarch and 1½ table-spoons cold water. Whisk the cornstarch mixture into the soup and cook for 3 minutes more over low heat.

Using tongs, place the noodles in the center of each soup bowl. Ladle the brothy vegetables over the top and serve at once.

YIELD: 4 TO 6 SERVINGS

### Shopping Tip

SHIITAKE MUSHROOMS, BOK CHOY, AND CHUKA SOBA NOODLES CAN BE FOUND IN ASIAN MARKETS, NATURAL FOOD STORES, AND WELL-STOCKED SUPERMARKETS.

### Some Like It Hotter

ADD 1 TO 2 TEASPOONS CHILI-GARLIC PASTE TO THE SOUP ALONG WITH THE SZECHUAN SAUCE.

# Vietnamese Pho Soup

PHO IS THE national soup of Vietnam (it means "your own bowl"). This version is filled with sprouts, snow peas, noodles, carrots, and wild mushrooms.

To make a vegetarian-style pho, substitute vegetable broth for chicken broth and use ½ pound extra-firm tofu instead of chicken.

½ ounce dried wood ear
   mushrooms
1 cup boiling water
1 tablespoon peanut oil
1 medium yellow onion, diced
2 teaspoons minced ginger root
1 or 2 Thai bird peppers or serrano
   peppers, seeded and minced
½ pound boneless chicken breasts or
   thighs, diced
5 cups chicken broth

2 carrots, thinly sliced at an angle
3 tablespoons soy sauce (preferably
   low sodium)
½ teaspoon black pepper
¼ pound snow peas, halved
2 tablespoons chopped cilantro
Juice of 1 lime
8 ounces rice noodles
2 large scallions, trimmed and
   chopped
2 ounces bean sprouts

IN A SMALL pan or mixing bowl, cover the dried mushrooms with the boiling water and set aside for 5 minutes. Drain and coarsely chop the reconstituted mushrooms.

In a large saucepan, heat the oil. Add the onion, ginger, and chili pepper and cook, stirring, for 3 minutes over medium heat. Add the chicken and cook, stirring, for 4 minutes more. Add the broth, carrots, soy sauce, black pepper, and mushrooms and bring to a simmer. Cook over medium heat for 10 minutes, stirring occasionally. Stir in the snow peas and cook for 10 minutes more. Stir in the cilantro and lime juice.

Meanwhile, in another large saucepan, bring 3 quarts of water to a boil over medium-high heat. Place the rice noodles in the boiling water, stir, and return to a boil. Cook until al dente, 4 to 5 minutes, stirring occasionally. Drain the noodles in a colander.

Place the cooked noodles in large soup bowls. Ladle the pho broth over the noodles. Arrange the scallions and bean sprouts over the top of each bowl and serve at once.

YIELD: 6 SERVINGS

**Shopping Tip**

DRIED WOOD EAR MUSHROOMS CAN BE FOUND IN ASIAN MARKETS, NATURAL FOOD STORES, AND WELL-STOCKED SUPERMARKETS. A MIXED GOURMET BLEND OF DRIED MUSHROOMS CAN ALSO BE USED.

# Chicken Firepot with Shiitake Mushrooms

THIS RIOTOUS CAULDRON is filled with fragrant ginger root, pungent soy sauce, earthy shiitake mushrooms, and prickly chili peppers.

For a subtle flavor variation, other exotic mushrooms, such as oyster or cremini mushrooms, can be used in place of the shiitakes.

1½ tablespoons canola oil

8 fresh shiitake mushrooms, sliced

8 to 10 domestic mushrooms, sliced

1 small red onion, chopped

4 cloves garlic, minced

1 tablespoon minced ginger root

2 or 3 serrano or Thai bird peppers, seeded and minced

¾ pound boneless chicken thighs, diced

4 cups chicken broth

2 carrots, thinly sliced at an angle

3 tablespoons soy sauce (preferably low sodium)

1 to 2 teaspoons sesame oil

½ teaspoon black pepper

2 cups chopped fresh spinach

¼ pound extra-firm tofu, diced

8 ounces lo mein or rice noodles

IN A LARGE saucepan, heat the oil. Add the shiitake and domestic mushrooms, onion, garlic, ginger, and chili peppers and cook, stirring, for 6 minutes over medium heat. Add the chicken and cook, stirring, for 4 minutes. Add the chicken broth, carrots, soy sauce, sesame oil, and black pepper and bring to a simmer. Cook for 15 minutes over medium heat, stirring occasionally. Stir in the spinach and tofu and return to a simmer. Cook for 5 minutes more, stirring occasionally.

Meanwhile, in a medium saucepan, bring about 2½ quarts of water to a boil over medium-high heat. Place the noodles in the boiling water, stir, and return to a boil. Cook until al dente, about 4 to 5 minutes, stirring occasionally. Drain the noodles in a colander.

Using tongs, transfer the noodles to shallow bowls. Ladle the soup over the top and serve at once.

YIELD: 6 SERVINGS

### Some Like It Hotter

ADD A FEW TEASPOONS OF CHILI-GARLIC PASTE TO THE BROTH WHILE IT SIMMERS.

# Pacific Noodle Soup

THIS BROTHY VEGETABLE soup captures the eclectic flavors of Pacific Rim cuisine.

This is a delicious soup to serve to your vegetarian guests.

1½ tablespoons canola oil

8 ounces mushrooms, sliced

1 small red onion, chopped

4 cloves garlic, minced

1 tablespoon minced ginger root

2 or 3 serrano or Thai bird peppers, seeded and minced

4 cups vegetable broth or chicken broth

2 carrots, thinly sliced at an angle

¼ pound snow peas, halved

3 tablespoons soy sauce (preferably low sodium)

2 teaspoons sesame oil

½ teaspoon black pepper

⅓ pound extra-firm tofu, diced

8 ounces udon or soba noodles

IN A LARGE saucepan, heat the oil. Add the mushrooms, onion, garlic, ginger, and chili peppers and cook, stirring, for 6 to 7 minutes over medium heat. Add the broth, carrots, snow peas, soy sauce, sesame oil, and black pepper and bring to a simmer. Cook for 12 to 15 minutes over medium heat, stirring occasionally. Stir in the tofu and cook for 5 minutes more.

Meanwhile, in a medium saucepan, bring about 2½ quarts of water to a boil over medium-high heat. Place the noodles in the boiling water, stir, and return to a boil. Cook until al dente, about 8 minutes, stirring occasionally. Drain the noodles in a colander.

Using tongs, place the noodles in shallow bowls. Ladle the soup and vegetables over the top and serve at once.

YIELD: 4 SERVINGS

🍴 *Shopping Tip*

UDON AND SUBA ARE AVAILABLE IN WELL-STOCKED SUPERMARKETS AND ASIAN GROCERY STORES.

🥄 *Spice Advice*

ADD 2 OR 3 TABLESPOONS MINCED CILANTRO TO THE BROTH NEAR THE FINISH. OR, TOP THE SOUP BOWLS WITH CHOPPED SCALLIONS AND/OR BEAN SPROUTS.

# Vegetable Dumplings in Chili Broth

VEGETABLE DUMPLINGS—little packages of shredded vegetables—add an exotic flair to this tingly hot soup.

1½ tablespoons canola oil

8 ounces mushrooms, sliced

1 small red onion, chopped

4 cloves garlic, minced

1 tablespoon minced ginger root

2 serrano or Thai bird peppers, seeded and minced

6 cups vegetable broth or water

2 carrots, thinly sliced at an angle

3 tablespoons soy sauce (preferably low sodium)

2 teaspoons sesame oil

12 frozen vegetable dumplings

¼ pound extra-firm tofu, diced

3 or 4 whole scallions, chopped

IN A LARGE saucepan, heat the oil. Add the mushrooms, onion, garlic, ginger, and chili peppers and cook, stirring, for 6 minutes over medium heat. Add the broth, carrots, soy sauce, and sesame oil and bring to a simmer. Cook for 15 minutes over medium heat, stirring occasionally.

Stir in the vegetable dumplings, tofu, and scallions and return to a simmer. Cook for 5 minutes over medium heat, stirring occasionally. Ladle the soup into bowls and serve at once.

YIELD: 6 SERVINGS

### Shopping Tip

VEGETABLE DUMPLINGS ARE AVAILABLE FRESH OR FROZEN IN ASIAN GROCERY STORES AND WELL-STOCKED SUPERMARKETS.

# Bang Pow Chicken Soup

THIS SOUP WILL have a knockout effect on your taste buds.

1½ tablespoons canola oil

8 ounces mushrooms, sliced

1 medium yellow onion, chopped

1 red bell pepper, seeded and diced

4 cloves garlic, minced

1 or 2 serrano or Thai bird peppers, seeded and minced

1 pound boneless chicken thighs, diced

4 cups chicken broth

1 can (8 ounces) sliced water chestnuts, drained

3 tablespoons soy sauce (preferably low sodium)

2 to 3 teaspoons chili-garlic paste

2 teaspoons sesame oil

½ teaspoon black pepper

2 cups coarsely chopped spinach or bok choy leaves

8 to 10 ounces lo mein or rice noodles

IN A LARGE saucepan, heat the oil. Add the mushrooms, onion, bell pepper, garlic, and chili pepper and cook, stirring, for 6 minutes over medium heat. Add the chicken and cook, stirring, for 4 minutes more. Add the chicken broth, water chestnuts, soy sauce, chili-garlic paste, sesame oil, and black pepper and bring to a simmer. Cook for 15 minutes over medium heat, stirring occasionally. Stir in the spinach and cook for 4 to 5 minutes more, stirring occasionally.

Meanwhile, in a medium saucepan bring about 2½ quarts of water to a boil over medium-high heat. Place the noodles in the boiling water, stir, and return to a boil. Cook until al dente, about 4 to 5 minutes, stirring occasionally. Drain the noodles in a colander.

Using tongs, transfer the noodles to shallow bowls. Ladle the soup over the top and serve at once.

YIELD: 6 SERVINGS

# Portobello Hot Pot with Curly Noodles

THIS VEGETARIAN BOWL is a cross between a stir-fry and Asian noodle soup. Woodsy portobello mushrooms are enhanced with soy sauce, chili-garlic paste, and sesame oil. Quick-cooking curly noodles soak up the flavors.

1 package (5 ounces) chuka soba
  noodles
1 tablespoon peanut oil
1 tablespoon rice vinegar
1 red bell pepper, seeded and cut into
  strips
¾ pound portobello mushrooms,
  trimmed and coarsely chopped
3 cloves garlic, minced

¼ pound snow peas, halved
¼ pound extra-firm tofu, diced
2 cups vegetable broth
3 tablespoons soy sauce (preferably
  low sodium)
2 teaspoons sesame oil
2 teaspoons chili-garlic paste
2 tablespoons peanut butter
2 teaspoons cornstarch

IN A LARGE saucepan, bring 2½ quarts of water to a boil over medium-high heat. Place the noodles in the boiling water. When the noodles rise to the top, gently stir and cook until al dente, about 5 minutes. Drain the noodles in a colander.

In a large saucepan or wok, heat the oil and vinegar over medium-high heat. Add the bell pepper, mushrooms, and garlic and stir-fry for about 6 minutes. Stir in the snow peas and tofu and stir-fry for 3 to 4 minutes more. Stir in the broth, soy sauce, sesame oil, and chili-garlic paste and bring to a simmer. Cook, stirring, for about 5 minutes. Reduce the heat to low and stir in the peanut butter.

Meanwhile, in a small bowl, combine the cornstarch with 2 teaspoons water. Whisk the cornstarch into the vegetable mixture and return to a simmer.

Using tongs, place the noodles in warm bowls and ladle the vegetables and broth over the top. Serve at once.

YIELD: 4 SERVINGS

### ℣ Shopping Tip

CHUKA SOBA NOODLES (ALSO CALLED JAPANESE CURLY NOODLES) ARE SOLD IN WELL-STOCKED SUPERMARKETS AND IN ASIAN GROCERY STORES. THEY ARE SIMILAR TO THE NOODLES USED IN COMMERCIAL RAMEN SOUPS.

# Thai Curry Scallops with Basil

THIS LIVELY CURRY is a mosaic of ginger, garlic, coconut, curry paste, and refreshing basil leaves.

1 tablespoon peanut oil

1 pound sea scallops

1 red bell pepper, cut into slivers

1 cup snow peas, halved

2 teaspoons minced ginger root

2 large cloves garlic, minced

2 teaspoons red or green curry
    paste

1 to 2 teaspoons chili-garlic paste
    (optional)

1 can (13½ ounces) coconut milk

3 to 4 tablespoons soy sauce
    (preferably low sodium)

8 to 10 fresh basil leaves

2 teaspoons cornstarch

4 cups cooked jasmine rice

IN A LARGE skillet or wok, heat the oil over medium-high heat. Add the scallops and stir-fry until opaque, about 7 minutes. Transfer the scallops to a warm plate.

Add the bell pepper to the pan and stir-fry for 3 minutes. Stir in the snow peas and stir-fry for 2 minutes more. Add the ginger and garlic and stir-fry over low heat for 2 minutes. Stir in the curry paste and optional chili-garlic paste and stir-fry for 30 seconds more. Stir in the coconut milk and soy sauce and bring to a gentle simmer over medium heat. Stir in the cooked scallops and basil leaves and return to a simmer. Cook, stirring, for 2 to 3 minutes over low heat.

Meanwhile, in a small mixing bowl, combine the cornstarch and 2 teaspoons water. Stir the cornstarch into the scallops mixture and cook, stirring, for 1 minute more.

Spoon the rice into large, wide bowls and ladle the scallops and sauce over the top. Serve at once.

YIELD: 4 SERVINGS

### ♈ Shopping Tip

RED AND GREEN CURRY PASTES, COCONUT MILK, JASMINE RICE, AND CHILI-GARLIC PASTE CAN BE FOUND IN ASIAN MARKETS AND WELL-STOCKED SUPERMARKETS. THAI PANANG CURRY CAN ALSO BE USED.

### ✖ Spice Advice

WHEN IN SEASON, INCLUDE THAI BASIL OR PURPLE BASIL IN THE DISH. THOSE HERBS HAVE STRONG UNDERTONES OF LICORICE AND PEPPER.

# Evil Jungle Peanut Chicken

THIS ADVENTUROUS CURRY dish lives up to its intriguing primal name.

1 tablespoon peanut oil

1¼ pounds boneless chicken breasts,
    diced

1 red bell pepper, seeded and cut
    into slivers

1 cup snow peas, halved

2 teaspoons minced lemon grass

2 teaspoons minced ginger root

2 cloves garlic, minced

2 teaspoons red or green curry paste

1 can (13½ ounces) coconut milk

3 tablespoons soy sauce (preferably
    low sodium)

3 tablespoons chunky peanut butter

1 to 2 teaspoons chili-garlic paste
    (optional)

6 to 8 fresh basil leaves

4 cups cooked jasmine rice

IN A LARGE skillet or wok, heat the oil over medium-high heat. Add the chicken and stir-fry until slightly browned and fully cooked, about 7 minutes. Remove the chicken to a warm plate.

Add the bell pepper to the skillet and stir-fry over medium heat for 3 minutes. Add the snow peas and stir-fry for 2 minutes more. Add the lemon grass, ginger, and garlic and stir-fry for 2 minutes more. Add the curry paste and stir-fry for 1 minute more. Add the coconut milk, soy sauce, peanut butter, and optional chili-garlic paste and bring to a gentle simmer. Add the cooked chicken and basil leaves and cook, stirring, for 3 minutes.

Spoon the rice into large, wide bowls. Ladle the chicken and sauce over the top. Serve at once.

YIELD: 4 SERVINGS

### ♦♦♦ Shopping Tip

RED AND GREEN CURRY PASTES, COCONUT MILK, JASMINE RICE, AND CHILI-GARLIC PASTE CAN BE FOUND IN ASIAN MARKETS AND WELL-STOCKED SUPERMARKETS. THAI PANANG CURRY CAN ALSO BE USED.

### ✦ Some Like It Hotter

ADD 2 JALAPEÑO OR SERRANO PEPPERS (SEEDED AND MINCED) TO THE PAN ALONG WITH THE LEMON GRASS.

# Masaman Curry Beef and Mushrooms

MASAMAN IS A dark Thai curry paste often paired with beef. Thai panang curry paste or red curry paste can also be used.

1 tablespoon peanut oil

1 pound top round or sirloin tip, cut into thin strips

1 red bell pepper, seeded and cut into slivers

8 ounces mushrooms, sliced

2 teaspoons minced ginger root

2 cloves garlic, minced

3 to 4 teaspoons masaman curry paste

1 cup canned coconut milk

1 cup chicken broth

½ pound snow peas, halved

3 tablespoons soy sauce (preferably low sodium)

1 teaspoon ground cumin

1 teaspoon ground coriander

1 tablespoon cornstarch

10 to 12 fresh basil leaves, cut into strips (optional)

4 cups cooked jasmine rice

IN A LARGE wok or saucepan, heat the oil over medium-high heat. Add the beef and stir-fry until browned, 4 to 6 minutes. Transfer to a plate and keep warm.

To the same wok, add the bell pepper and mushrooms and stir-fry over medium heat for 5 minutes. Add the ginger and garlic and stir-fry for 2 minutes. Add the beef and curry paste and stir-fry for 2 minutes more. Stir in the coconut milk, broth, snow peas, soy sauce, cumin, and coriander and bring to a gentle simmer over medium heat. Cook, stirring, for about 5 minutes.

Meanwhile, in a small mixing bowl, combine the cornstarch with 1 tablespoon water. Whisk the cornstarch into the curry sauce and cook, stirring, for 1 minute. Stir in the optional basil leaves.

Spoon the rice into large, wide bowls. Ladle the beef curry over the top of the rice and serve at once.

YIELD: 4 SERVINGS

### ▯▯▯ Shopping Tip

MASAMAN CURRY PASTE, COCONUT MILK, AND JASMINE RICE ARE AVAILABLE IN ASIAN GROCERY STORES AND WELL-STOCKED SUPERMARKETS.

### Some Like It Hotter

ADD 2 TEASPOONS CHILI-GARLIC PASTE ALONG WITH THE CURRY PASTE.

# Red Curry Vegetables

CHILI-GARLIC PASTE and red curry paste deliver a double dose of fire in this stir-fried bowl of vegetables and coconut sauce. Curry paste and coconut milk are a delicious combination.

| | |
|---|---|
| 1 tablespoon peanut oil | ¾ cup vegetable broth |
| 1 red bell pepper, seeded and cut into slivers | 3 tablespoons soy sauce (preferably low sodium) |
| 12 ounces mushrooms, sliced | 2 teaspoons sesame oil |
| 2 cloves garlic, minced | ¼ pound extra-firm tofu, diced |
| 2 teaspoons red curry paste | 12 broccoli florets |
| 1 or 2 teaspoons chili-garlic paste | 1 tablespoon cornstarch |
| 1 cup canned coconut milk | 4 cups cooked jasmine or basmati rice |

IN A LARGE skillet or wok, heat the oil over medium-high heat. Add the bell pepper and mushrooms and stir-fry for 4 to 5 minutes. Add the garlic and stir-fry for 2 minutes more. Add the curry paste and chili-garlic paste and stir-fry for 2 minutes more. Add the coconut milk, broth, soy sauce, and sesame oil and bring to a gentle simmer over medium heat. Stir in the tofu and broccoli and cook, stirring, for about 5 minutes.

Meanwhile, in a small mixing bowl, combine the cornstarch with 1 tablespoon water. Stir the cornstarch into the curried vegetables and cook, stirring, for 1 minute.

Spoon the rice into large, wide bowls and ladle the curried vegetables over the top. Serve at once.

YIELD: 4 SERVINGS

### ▯▯▯ Shopping Tip

RED CURRY PASTE, JASMINE RICE, AND CANNED COCONUT MILK ARE AVAILABLE IN ASIAN GROCERY STORES AND IN WELL-STOCKED SUPERMARKETS. BASMATI RICE CAN BE SUBSTITUTED FOR JASMINE RICE.

# Thai Fragrant Shrimp and Chicken Pot

THIS CAULDRON IS imbued with herbal and piquant flavors.

1 tablespoon peanut oil

½ pound boneless chicken thighs,
    diced

1 tablespoon minced lemon grass

4 cloves garlic, minced

2 Thai bird peppers, seeded and
    minced

4 cups chicken broth

4 whole scallions, chopped

2 cups shredded bok choy

1 carrot, thinly sliced at an angle

2 to 3 tablespoons soy sauce
    (preferably low sodium)

Juice of 1 lime

½ pound medium shrimp, peeled and
    deveined

2 tablespoons chopped fresh cilantro

4 ounces cellophane or rice vermicelli

IN A LARGE saucepan, heat the oil over medium-high heat. Add the chicken and cook, stirring, until fully cooked, 8 to 10 minutes. Add the lemon grass, garlic, and chili peppers and cook, stirring, over medium heat for 2 to 3 minutes. Add the chicken broth, scallions, bok choy, carrot, soy sauce, and lime juice and bring to a simmer. Add the shrimp and cook over medium heat for 12 to 15 minutes until the shrimp are fully cooked, stirring occasionally. Add the cilantro and cook for 2 minutes over medium-low heat.

Meanwhile, in a medium saucepan filled with boiling water, add the cellophane noodles; cook for 3 minutes over medium heat, stirring occasionally. Drain the noodles in a colander.

Using tongs or a large slotted spoon, place the noodles in soup bowls. Ladle the soup over the noodles and serve at once.

YIELD: 6 SERVINGS

# CHAPTER NINE

# When Worlds Collide

## GLOBAL MELTING POTS

ONE OF THE hallmarks of hot-and-spicy cuisine is that it encourages culinary improvisation and inventive twists. Chili peppers are not confined to ethnic dishes; rather, the peppery pods enhance a variety of one-pot dishes from around the world. Time and again, one or two chili peppers, along with a brigade of spices, will bring a taste of sunshine and blue skies to a traditionally mild, humdrum dish. With chili peppers in the kitchen, all is well.

This chapter highlights the use of chili peppers in nontraditional recipes. In winsome creations such as Red Pepper Vichyssoise, Champagne Chili Risotto, and Ginger-Dill Borscht, chili peppers heighten and brighten without overpowering the meals. Cross-cultural recipes such as Southwestern Pasta Fazool, Chili Matzo Ball Soup, and Mexican Minestrone display the versatility of chili peppers while offering new dimensions to old-world classics.

With chili pepper–inspired melting pots, there are no borders, barriers, or rules of engagement. A willingness to explore and experiment are the only tenets of this chapter. The goal is to prepare well-balanced dishes with high-impact flavors. Hopefully, the results will be triumphant.

# Red Pepper Vichyssoise

THIS ADAPTATION OF the classic creamy potato bisque marries the sweet essence of red bell peppers with the tingly hot sensation of hot chili peppers.

| | |
|---|---|
| 1 tablespoon canola oil | 2 tablespoons dry white wine |
| 2 red bell peppers, seeded and diced | 2 teaspoons dried parsley |
| 1 medium yellow onion, diced | 1 teaspoon dried thyme |
| 1 large stalk celery, diced | 1 teaspoon paprika |
| 3 or 4 cloves garlic, minced | ½ teaspoon white pepper |
| 1 or 2 red Fresno or red jalapeño peppers, seeded and minced | ½ teaspoon salt |
| 2 cups peeled, diced potatoes | 1 cup whole milk or light cream |

IN A LARGE saucepan, heat the oil. Add the bell peppers, onion, celery, garlic, and chili pepper and cook, stirring, for 6 minutes over medium-high heat. Add 4 cups water, the potatoes, wine, parsley, thyme, paprika, white pepper, and salt and bring to a simmer. Cook for 20 to 25 minutes over medium-low heat, stirring occasionally, until the potatoes are tender.

Transfer the soup to a food processor fitted with a steel blade or to a blender and process until smooth, about 5 seconds. Return to the pan and stir in the milk. Bring to a gentle simmer over medium heat.

Ladle the vichyssoise into bowls and serve hot with warm French bread.

YIELD: 6 SERVINGS

# Asparagus Chili Bisque

THIS REGAL ASPARAGUS bisque is heightened with the distinctive presence of dried chili peppers.

| | |
|---|---|
| 3 or 4 guajillo or dried New Mexico chilies | ½ teaspoon white pepper |
| | ½ teaspoon salt |
| 1 cup simmering water | 1¼ pounds asparagus spears, trimmed and cut into ½-inch pieces |
| 1 tablespoon canola oil | |
| 1 medium yellow onion, diced | 1 cup milk or light cream |
| 3 or 4 cloves garlic, minced | ½ cup shredded Monterey Jack cheese |
| 2 cups peeled, diced potatoes | 2 to 3 tablespoons chopped fresh parsley |

COVER THE CHILIES with the simmering water and soak until soft, about 15 to 20 minutes. Place a lid (or plate) over the chilies to keep them from floating. Drain the chilies, reserving ½ cup liquid. Remove the seeds and chop the flesh.

In a large saucepan, heat the oil. Add the onion and garlic and cook, stirring, for 4 to 5 minutes over medium-high heat. Add 4 cups water, the potatoes, white pepper, and salt and bring to a simmer. Cook over medium heat for about 10 minutes, stirring occasionally. Add the asparagus, chilies, and reserved liquid and cook for 15 minutes more, stirring occasionally.

Transfer the soup to a blender or a food processor fitted with a steel blade and puree until smooth. Return the soup to the pan and stir in the milk, cheese, and parsley and return to a gentle simmer. Remove from the heat and ladle into bowls.

YIELD: 6 SERVINGS

# Country Split Pea Soup with Portobello Mushrooms

THIS INVITING VERSION of split pea soup is fortified with chewy portobello mushrooms and perky jalapeño peppers.

| | |
|---|---|
| 1½ tablespoons canola oil | 4 cloves garlic, minced |
| 1 large yellow onion, diced | 1 cup dried green split peas |
| 2 stalks celery, chopped | 2 cups diced potatoes |
| 2 medium portobello mushroom caps, coarsely chopped | 1 tablespoon dried parsley |
| | 1 tablespoon dried oregano |
| 2 jalapeño peppers, seeded and minced | 1 teaspoon black pepper |
| | 1 teaspoon salt |

IN A LARGE saucepan, heat the oil. Add the onion, celery, mushrooms, jalapeño peppers, and garlic and cook, stirring, for 8 minutes over medium-high heat. Add 8 cups water and the split peas and bring to a simmer. Cook for about 30 minutes over medium heat, stirring occasionally. Stir in the potatoes, parsley, oregano, black pepper and cook for about 1 hour until the split peas are tender, stirring occasionally.

Stir in the salt and remove from the heat. Let stand for 5 to 10 minutes before serving. Ladle into bowls and serve with whole grain bread.

YIELD: 6 SERVINGS

### ¶¶¶ Shopping Tip

PORTOBELLO MUSHROOMS ARE AVAILABLE IN THE PRODUCE SECTION OF WELL-STOCKED SUPERMARKETS.

# Ginger-Dill Borscht

THE HUMBLE BEET is transformed into a magenta-hued gourmet bisque.

1 tablespoon canola oil

1 medium yellow onion, diced

4 cloves garlic, minced

2 tablespoons minced ginger root

1 jalapeño or red Fresno pepper,
    seeded and minced

2 cups diced fresh beets, scrubbed
    (2 or 3 beets)

1 cup diced sweet potatoes

2 tablespoons dry red wine

1 tablespoon dried parsley

2 teaspoons dried dill weed

½ teaspoon black pepper

½ teaspoon salt

¼ cup lowfat plain yogurt

IN A LARGE saucepan, heat the oil. Add the onion, garlic, ginger, and chili pepper and cook, stirring, for 4 minutes over medium-high heat. Add 5 cups water, the beets, sweet potatoes, wine, parsley, dill, black pepper, and salt and bring to a simmer. Cook over medium heat until the beets are tender, about 45 minutes, stirring occasionally.

Transfer the mixture to a food processor fitted with a steel blade or to a blender and process until smooth, about 5 seconds. Return to the pan.

Ladle the borscht into bowls. Swirl a tablespoon of yogurt in the center of each bowl and serve at once.

YIELD: 4 SERVINGS

## Spice Advice

IF USING FRESH DILL, ADD ABOUT 1½ TABLESPOONS (CHOPPED) TO THE BORSCHT ABOUT 5 TO 10 MINUTES BEFORE THE END OF THE COOKING TIME.

# Mexican Minestrone

CORN MACARONI, MADE with corn flour, imbues this minestrone with Mexican flavor.

1 tablespoon canola oil

1 medium yellow onion, diced

1 red or green bell pepper, seeded and
    diced

4 cloves garlic, minced

1 jalapeño or canned chipotle pepper,
    seeded and minced

6 cups vegetable broth

¼ cup canned tomato paste

2 teaspoons dried oregano

1½ teaspoons ground cumin

½ teaspoon black pepper

½ teaspoon salt

1 cup corn macaroni or elbow
    macaroni

1½ cups corn kernels, fresh or
    frozen

1 cup cooked or canned (drained)
    black beans

¼ cup chopped fresh parsley

IN A LARGE saucepan, heat the oil. Add the onion, bell pepper, garlic, and chili pepper and cook, stirring, for 6 minutes over medium-high heat. Stir in the broth, tomato paste, oregano, cumin, black pepper, and salt and bring to a simmer. Cook for 7 minutes over medium heat, stirring occasionally. Stir in the macaroni, corn, beans, and parsley and return to a simmer. Cook for 5 to 7 minutes over medium-high heat, stirring occasionally, until the pasta is al dente.

Remove from the heat and let stand for 5 minutes before serving.

Ladle the minestrone into shallow bowls and serve at once with warm flour tortillas.

YIELD: 6 SERVINGS

🍴 *Shopping Tip*

CORN MACARONI IS AVAILABLE
IN THE GOURMET PASTA SECTION
OF MOST SUPERMARKETS AND
SPECIALTY FOOD STORES.

🥄 *Spice Advice*

STIR IN 2 TO 3 TABLESPOONS
CHOPPED CILANTRO NEAR
THE FINISH.

# Chili Matzo Ball Soup

MATZO BALL SOUP is the ultimate comfort food. This sprightly version includes spring vegetables and chili-enhanced matzo balls (dumplings made with matzo meal).

| | |
|---|---|
| 3 large eggs | 2 cups coarsely chopped leeks |
| 4 tablespoons canola oil | 1 red bell pepper, seeded and diced |
| 1 cup matzo meal | 2 or 3 cloves garlic, minced |
| 1 tablespoon chopped pickled jalapeños | 6 cups chicken broth or vegetable broth |
| 2 teaspoons salt | 2 large carrots, diced |
| 1 medium yellow onion, diced | ½ teaspoon black pepper |

To MAKE THE matzo balls, beat the eggs in a medium mixing bowl. Add 3 tablespoons of the oil and beat again. Fold in the matzo meal, pickled jalapeños, and 1 teaspoon of the salt. Blend in 3 tablespoons water, cover the dough, and refrigerate for about 15 minutes.

In a large saucepan, bring about 2 quarts of water to a boil. Remove the matzo dough from the refrigerator. Using moistened hands, form 8 dumplings about the size of golf balls and drop into the boiling water. Cover the pan and cook over medium heat for about 20 minutes, stirring the balls occasionally. Drain the dumplings and discard the liquid. Set aside until the soup is ready.

In a large saucepan, heat the remaining 1 tablespoon oil. Add the onion, leeks, bell pepper, and garlic and cook, stirring, for 6 to 7 minutes over medium heat. Add the broth, carrots, black pepper, and remaining 1 teaspoon salt and bring to a simmer. Cook over medium-low heat for

15 minutes, stirring occasionally. Add the cooked matzo balls and return to a simmer. Cook for 10 to 15 minutes more over medium-low heat, stirring occasionally.

Place a matzo ball in the center of each bowl and ladle the brothy vegetables over the top.

YIELD: 6 SERVINGS

### ¶¶¶ Shopping Tip

MATZO MEAL IS AVAILABLE IN

THE ETHNIC SECTIONS OF

WELL-STOCKED SUPERMARKETS.

# Mediterranean Swordfish Cioppino

GARDEN HERBS AND feisty chili peppers provide this traditional seafood stew with appetizing flavors and aromas.

Other firm-textured fish, such as marlin, grouper, or shark, can be used in place of the swordfish. As with any fish, be careful of tiny bones.

1 tablespoon canola oil

1 medium yellow onion, diced

1 green bell pepper, seeded and diced

4 cloves garlic, minced

2 jalapeño or serrano peppers, seeded and minced

3 cups fish stock or clam juice

1 can (14 ounces) stewed tomatoes or plum tomatoes

¼ cup dry red wine

2 teaspoons dried oregano

1 teaspoon dried basil

½ teaspoon black pepper

½ teaspoon salt

¾ pound fresh swordfish steak, cubed

½ pound sea scallops or medium shrimp, peeled and deveined

¼ cup tomato paste

¼ cup chopped fresh parsley

IN A LARGE saucepan, heat the oil. Add the onion, bell pepper, garlic, and chili peppers and cook, stirring, for 5 minutes over medium-high heat. Add the fish stock, stewed tomatoes, wine, oregano, basil, black pepper, and salt and bring to a simmer. Cook for 10 minutes over medium heat, stirring occasionally.

Add the swordfish and scallops and return to a simmer. Cook for 15 minutes over medium heat, stirring occasionally. Stir in the tomato paste and parsley and cook for 5 minutes more.

Ladle the stew into shallow bowls and serve at once with warm French bread.

YIELD: 4 SERVINGS

### Some Like It Hotter

JUST BEFORE SERVING,
LIBERALLY ADD BOTTLED RED
HOT SAUCE TO THE STEW.

# Triple Chili Ratatouille

A BARRAGE OF hot spices reinvigorates this Mediterranean vegetable stew.

2 tablespoons canola oil

1 medium yellow onion, diced

1 medium zucchini, diced

2 cups diced eggplant

4 cloves garlic, minced

1 or 2 jalapeño peppers, seeded and minced

1 can (28 ounces) plum tomatoes

1 can (15 ounces) red or white kidney beans, drained

1 canned chipotle pepper, seeded and minced

1 tablespoon dried parsley

2 teaspoons dried oregano

½ teaspoon cayenne pepper

½ teaspoon salt

½ teaspoon red pepper flakes

IN A LARGE saucepan, heat the oil. Add the onion, zucchini, eggplant, garlic, and jalapeño pepper and cook, stirring, for 8 to 10 minutes over medium heat. Add the plum tomatoes, beans, chipotle pepper, parsley, oregano, cayenne pepper, salt, and red pepper flakes and bring to a simmer. Cook over medium-low heat for 15 minutes, stirring occasionally. Cut the plum tomatoes into smaller pieces with the edge of a spoon as the stew cooks.

Remove the ratatouille from the heat and let stand for 5 minutes. Serve in large bowls with pasta or rice as a bed.

YIELD: 4 SERVINGS

### Shopping Tip

LOOK FOR CANNED CHIPOTLE PEPPERS IN MEXICAN GROCERY STORES AND WELL-STOCKED SUPERMARKETS.

# Champagne Chili Risotto

RISOTTO, THE LUSCIOUS Italian dish, is made with arborio rice, a cooked grain that turns creamy, not fluffy. Jalapeños give this risotto a spicy personality.

1½ tablespoons canola oil or olive oil

12 ounces mushrooms, sliced

1 medium yellow onion, chopped

4 cloves garlic, minced

1 to 2 tablespoons minced pickled
    jalapeños

1½ cups arborio rice

½ cup dry champagne or white
    wine

½ teaspoon turmeric

½ teaspoon white pepper

½ teaspoon salt

1 cup frozen green peas

½ cup grated Parmesan cheese

IN A LARGE saucepan, heat the oil. Add the mushrooms, onion, and garlic and cook, stirring, for 7 minutes over medium heat. Stir in the pickled jalapeños and cook, stirring, for 1 minute more. Stir in the rice, 2 cups water, the champagne, turmeric, white pepper, and salt and bring to a simmer. Cook, stirring (uncovered), over medium heat for about 10 minutes.

Stir in 2½ cups water and the peas and cook over medium-low heat until all of the liquid is absorbed, about 12 minutes, stirring frequently. Remove from the heat and stir in the cheese. Spoon the risotto into shallow bowls and serve with warm Italian bread.

YIELD: 4 SERVINGS

### Some Like It Hotter

ADD 2 OR 3 WHOLE SERRANO CHILIES ALONG
WITH THE RICE. REMOVE AT THE FINISH AND
SERVE THE CHILIES ON THE SIDE.

# Southwestern Pasta Fazool

NEW MEXICO MEETS Italy in this colorful melange of black beans, pasta, corn, herbs, and hot peppers.

For a variation in color, other canned beans, such as pinto beans or pink beans, can be used in place of the black beans.

| | |
|---|---|
| 1 tablespoon canola oil | 1½ teaspoons ground cumin |
| 1 medium yellow onion, diced | ½ teaspoon black pepper |
| 1 red or green bell pepper, seeded and diced | ½ teaspoon salt |
| 4 cloves garlic, minced | 1 cup corn macaroni or elbow macaroni |
| 2 jalapeño peppers, seeded and minced | 1 can (11 ounces) corn kernels, drained |
| 6 cups vegetable broth | 1 cup canned black beans or red kidney beans |
| 2 cups diced sweet potato | ¼ cup chopped fresh parsley (optional) |
| ¼ cup tomato paste | |
| 2 teaspoons dried oregano | |

IN A LARGE saucepan, heat the oil. Add the onion, bell pepper, garlic, and jalapeño peppers and cook, stirring, for 7 minutes over medium-high heat. Add the broth, sweet potato, tomato paste, oregano, cumin, black pepper, and salt and bring to a simmer. Cook for 12 to 15 minutes over medium heat, stirring occasionally.

Stir in the macaroni, corn, beans, and optional parsley and return to a simmer. Cook over medium heat until the pasta is al dente, about 5 to 7 minutes, stirring occasionally. Remove from the heat and let stand for 5 to 10 minutes before serving.

Ladle the soup into bowls and serve at once with plenty of warm flour tortillas.

YIELD: 6 SERVINGS

### 🍴 Shopping Tip

CORN MACARONI IS AVAILABLE
IN THE GOURMET PASTA
SECTION OF WELL-STOCKED
SUPERMARKETS AND IN
SPECIALTY FOOD STORES.

### ✗ Spice Advice

ADD 2 TABLESPOONS CHOPPED
CILANTRO AT THE FINISH.
SHREDDED MONTEREY JACK
CHEESE MAKES A NICE TOPPING.

# Peppery Yellow Pilaf

THIS BRIGHTLY FLAVORED dish radiates with sweet peppers and hot chilies.

1 tablespoon canola oil

1 medium yellow onion, diced

1 red bell pepper, seeded and diced

3 or 4 cloves garlic, minced

1 or 2 jalapeño peppers, seeded and minced

1 red cherry pepper, seeded and minced

2 cups peeled, diced butternut squash

1½ cups long-grain white rice

½ teaspoon turmeric

½ teaspoon black pepper

½ teaspoon salt

¼ teaspoon cayenne pepper

IN A MEDIUM saucepan, heat the oil. Add the onion, bell pepper, garlic, and jalapeño and cherry peppers and cook, stirring, for 5 minutes over medium heat. Stir in 3 cups water, the squash, rice, turmeric, black pepper, salt, and cayenne pepper and bring to a simmer. Stir the grains, cover, and cook over medium-low heat until the rice and squash are tender, about 15 to 20 minutes.

Fluff the rice and let stand (still covered) for about 5 minutes. Transfer to a large serving bowl and serve as a spicy side dish.

YIELD: 6 SERVINGS

### Shopping Tip

CHERRY PEPPERS ARE SMALL, BULBOUS CHILI PEPPERS THAT RANGE FROM MILD TO TINGLY HOT. THEY ARE AVAILABLE ON A SEASONAL BASIS AT FARMERS' MARKETS AND IN SUPERMARKETS.

# Vermicelli Jalapeño Pilaf

THIS MIDDLE EASTERN dish of rice, noodles, chicken, and chick-peas is jazzed up with versatile jalapeño peppers.

½ pound vermicelli or angel hair pasta

2 tablespoons canola oil

1 tablespoon olive oil

1 medium yellow onion, finely chopped

2 cloves garlic, minced

¾ pound boneless chicken thighs or
    breasts, diced

4 cups chicken broth or water

1½ cups long-grain white rice

1 can (15 ounces) chick-peas, drained

2 tablespoons chopped pickled
    jalapeños

½ teaspoon turmeric

½ teaspoon ground cumin

½ teaspoon black pepper

½ teaspoon salt

BREAK THE VERMICELLI into small pieces (this can be done over a large bowl with your hands). Heat the canola oil in a large skillet and add the vermicelli. Cook, stirring, over medium heat until the noodles are golden brown, about 10 minutes. Remove from the heat. (Toasting the noodles in a skillet brings out a nutty flavor.)

In a large saucepan, heat the olive oil. Add the onion and garlic and cook over medium heat, stirring, for 4 minutes. Add the chicken and cook, stirring, until the chicken is browned, about 6 minutes. Stir in the broth, rice, chick-peas, pickled jalapeños, turmeric, cumin, black pepper, salt, and toasted vermicelli and bring to a simmer. Cover the pan and cook over medium-low heat until all of the liquid is absorbed, about 15 to 20 minutes.

Fluff the pilaf and let stand for 5 to 10 minutes before serving.

YIELD: 6 SERVINGS

# Cheese Tortellini with Diablo Ragù

"DIABLO," OR "DIAVOLO," loosely means "devil" in Italian, as in "devilishly hot."

1 tablespoon canola oil

2 large carrots, chopped

1 medium yellow onion, diced

1 large stalk celery, diced

2 large cloves garlic, minced

1 can (28 ounces) stewed tomatoes or
    plum tomatoes

2 tablespoons tomato paste

2 tablespoons chopped pickled
    pepperoncinis

1 tablespoon dried parsley

2 teaspoons dried oregano

¼ to ½ teaspoon red pepper flakes

8 to 12 ounces dried cheese tortellini

IN A LARGE saucepan, heat the oil. Add the carrots, onion, celery, and garlic and cook, stirring, for 6 to 7 minutes over medium heat. Add the stewed tomatoes, tomato paste, pepperoncinis, parsley, oregano, and red pepper flakes and bring to a simmer. Cook for about 15 minutes over medium-low heat, stirring occasionally. As the sauce cooks, use the edge of a spoon to cut the chunks of tomatoes into smaller pieces.

Meanwhile, in a large saucepan, bring 4 quarts of water to a boil over medium-high heat. Place the tortellini in the boiling water, stir, and return to a boil. Cook until al dente, 8 to 10 minutes, stirring occasionally. Drain in a colander.

Place the tortellini in bowls and ladle the sauce over the top. Serve with Italian bread to mop up the sauce.

YIELD: 4 SERVINGS

# Small Bowls with Big Flavors

## DIPS AND SPREADS

A BOWL FILLED with a dip has the table all to itself. Informal, unpretentious, and meant to be shared by all, scrumptious dips and spreads serve to stimulate the taste buds for the meal to come—and they sometimes steal the show. More than once, a tasty salsa or feisty guacamole has rescued a drifting cocktail party from the meandering doldrums. Without a doubt, a savory dip can be the hit of the party.

This chapter features a variety of dips, such as Tempting Tomato Salsa, Roasted Chili Hummus, Jalapeño Black Bean Dip, and one of my all-time favorites, Jay's Papaya Guacamole. These are simple yet exuberantly flavored bowls for dipping, for spreading, or, when no one is watching, to be eaten by the spoonful. This chapter offers further proof that some of the best edible things in life come in a bowl.

When serving dips and spreads, offer a selection of tortilla chips, pita bread wedges, and cut-up vegetables, such as carrots, broccoli florets, and celery. Serving fancy tortilla chips flavored with black beans, blue corn, or dried vegetables can also enhance the meal (and impress your friends at the same time). Don't shy away from doubling a recipe, as a great dip or spread can always be eaten the next day as well.

# Sweet Pepper Rouille

THIS PROVENÇAL "bread sauce" offers a spectrum of sweet, piquant, and herbal flavors. Serve it in a bowl as a dip, spread it on a sandwich, or smother it over barbecued chicken or fish.

*4 thick slices of French or Italian bread, crusts removed*

*1 cup diced roasted sweet peppers*

*2 tablespoons olive oil*

*2 cloves garlic, minced*

*3 to 4 tablespoons chopped fresh parsley*

*1 or 2 serrano peppers, seeded and minced*

*½ teaspoon dried thyme*

*½ teaspoon salt*

*¼ teaspoon cayenne pepper*

IN A MEDIUM mixing bowl, soak the bread in warm water for about 5 seconds. Place the bread in a colander, drain, and gently squeeze out the excess water (like a sponge).

Transfer the bread to a blender or a food processor fitted with a steel blade. Add the sweet peppers, oil, garlic, parsley, serrano peppers, thyme, salt, and cayenne pepper. Process the mixture until smooth, about 5 seconds. Transfer to a serving bowl.

YIELD: 2 CUPS

# Roasted Chili Hummus

ROASTED CHILI PEPPERS transform humdrum hummus into an exciting dip.

2 fresh New Mexico or poblano
   chilies, cored and seeded

1 can (15 ounces) chick-peas

¼ cup tahini (sesame seed paste)

Juice of 1 lemon

2 large cloves garlic, minced

¼ cup chopped fresh parsley

1 teaspoon ground cumin

½ teaspoon cayenne pepper

½ teaspoon salt

ROAST THE CHILIES by placing them over an open flame or beneath a preheated broiler for 4 to 6 minutes on each side until the skin is charred. Remove the chilies from the heat and let cool for a few minutes. Using a butter knife, scrape the charred skin from the flesh and discard. Remove the seeds and chop the flesh.

Drain the chick-peas, reserving about ¼ cup of the liquid. Place the roasted chilies, chick-peas with their liquid, tahini, lemon juice, garlic, parsley, cumin, cayenne pepper, and salt in a food processor fitted with a steel blade or in a blender and process until smooth, about 10 seconds. Stop to scrape the sides with a spatula at least once.

Transfer the hummus to a serving bowl and serve with warm pita bread and/or raw vegetables. Hummus also makes a tasty sandwich spread.

YIELD: 2 CUPS

# Jalapeño Black Bean Dip

THIS APPETIZING BEAN dip is so tasty, you will be tempted to eat it by the spoonful.

| | |
|---|---|
| 1 can (15 ounces) black beans | 2 cloves garlic, minced |
| 1 tablespoon canola oil | 2 whole scallions, trimmed and |
| 1 small yellow onion, diced | chopped |
| 1 medium tomato, diced | 1½ teaspoons dried oregano |
| 2 tablespoons chopped pickled | 1 teaspoon ground cumin |
| jalapeños | ½ teaspoon black pepper |

DRAIN THE BEANS, reserving ¼ cup of the liquid.

In a medium saucepan, heat the oil. Add the onion, tomato, pickled jalapeños, and garlic and cook, stirring, for 5 minutes over medium heat. Add the beans with their liquid, the scallions, oregano, cumin, and black pepper and cook for about 7 minutes, stirring occasionally.

Transfer the mixture to a food processor fitted with a steel blade or to a blender and process until smooth, about 5 seconds. Pour the pureed beans into a serving bowl. Serve as a dip with warm flour tortillas, pita bread, or cut-up vegetables.

YIELD: ABOUT 2 CUPS

# Tempting Tomato Salsa

THIS PEPPERY TOMATO dip is a most versatile and flavorful salsa. Swoosh a chip into it or serve it alongside burritos or quesadillas.

2 large plum tomatoes, diced

1 green bell pepper, seeded and diced

1 medium yellow onion, diced

2 cloves garlic, minced

2 tablespoons minced pickled
    jalapeños

1 serrano pepper, seeded and minced
    (optional)

2 tablespoons chopped fresh cilantro

Juice of 1 lime

2 teaspoons dried oregano

1 teaspoon ground cumin

½ teaspoon cayenne pepper

½ teaspoon black pepper

½ teaspoon salt

1 can (16 ounces) crushed
    tomatoes

1 to 3 teaspoons bottled hot sauce

IN A LARGE mixing bowl, blend together all of the ingredients. Place three-quarters of the mixture in a blender or food processor fitted with a steel blade and process for 5 seconds, creating a chunky vegetable mash.

Return the pureed vegetables to the bowl and blend together again. Transfer the salsa to a bowl and chill for 15 to 30 minutes to allow the flavors to meld. Serve with warm flour tortillas or as a condiment for burritos or quesadillas.

YIELD: 4 CUPS (ABOUT 12 SERVINGS)

# Salsa Verde

SALSA VERDE, WHICH means "green sauce," is a mellifluous, smooth-textured sauce of tomatillos, cilantro, and green chilies. It makes a wonderful table companion to tomato salsa and guacamole.

1 tablespoon canola oil

1 small yellow onion, diced

2 cloves garlic, minced

1 can (12 ounces) whole tomatillos, drained

¾ cup vegetable broth

1 to 2 tablespoons minced pickled jalapeño or serrano chilies

½ teaspoon ground cumin

½ teaspoon black pepper

½ teaspoon salt

2 tablespoons chopped fresh cilantro

IN A MEDIUM saucepan, heat the oil. Add the onion and garlic and cook, stirring, for 3 to 4 minutes over medium-high heat. Add the tomatillos, broth, pickled chilies, cumin, black pepper, and salt and bring to a simmer. Cook, stirring, for 7 minutes over medium heat.

Transfer the mixture to a blender or food processor fitted with a steel blade and process until smooth, about 5 seconds. Return to the pan and cook, stirring, for about 10 minutes more over medium-low heat. Stir in the cilantro and transfer to a bowl. Serve the sauce with tortilla-based dishes (such as burritos) or as a dip. Refrigerate any leftover sauce for later use.

YIELD: 1½ CUPS

### ♈ Shopping Tip

CANNED TOMATILLOS ARE AVAILABLE IN WELL-STOCKED SUPERMARKETS AND IN MEXICAN GROCERY STORES.

# Jay's Papaya Guacamole

THIS MARRIAGE OF papayas and avocados is a match made in heaven. You'll want to gobble this up by the spoonful!

2 ripe avocados, peeled, pitted, and
   chopped

1 papaya, peeled, halved, seeded, and
   chopped

1 large tomato, diced

¼ cup finely chopped red onion

2 cloves garlic, minced

2 tablespoons chopped fresh cilantro

Juice of 1 lime

½ teaspoon ground cumin

½ teaspoon salt

½ teaspoon black pepper

2 scallions, chopped

1 to 3 teaspoons bottled red hot sauce

PLACE THE AVOCADOS, papaya, tomato, red onion, garlic, cilantro, lime juice, cumin, salt, black pepper, and hot sauce in a food processor fitted with a steel blade or in a blender and process until chunky-smooth, about 5 seconds. (Alternatively, mash the ingredients with a large spoon in a mixing bowl until a chunky paste is formed.)

Transfer the guacamole to a serving bowl and top with scallions. Serve as a dip with tortilla chips or vegetables.

YIELD: 4 TO 6 SERVINGS

## Shopping Tip

FOR THE BEST GUACAMOLE, USE RIPE AVOCADOS. YOU CAN DETERMINE AN AVOCADO'S RIPENESS BY HOLDING IT IN THE BASE OF YOUR HAND AND PRESSING DOWN LIGHTLY WITH YOUR THUMB; IT SHOULD GIVE A LITTLE.

# Chili Pepper Skordalia

SKORDALIA IS A garlicky potato sauce rooted in Greek cuisine. This zesty version can be served as a dip or sauce for vegetables, chicken, or beans.

2½ cups peeled, diced potatoes

2 poblano or fresh New Mexico chilies, cored and seeded

4 cloves garlic, chopped

¼ cup olive oil

3 tablespoons rice vinegar

1 tablespoon lemon juice

½ teaspoon salt

½ teaspoon white pepper

PLACE THE POTATOES in boiling water to cover and cook over medium heat until easily pierced with a fork, about 20 minutes. Drain in a colander.

Meanwhile, roast the chilies by placing them over an open flame or beneath a preheated broiler for 4 to 6 minutes on each side until the skin is charred. Remove the chilies from the heat and let cool for a few minutes. Using a butter knife, scrape the charred skin from the flesh and discard. Remove the seeds and chop the flesh.

Place the garlic in a food processor fitted with a steel blade or in a blender and process until minced, about 5 seconds. Add the potatoes, roasted peppers, oil, vinegar, lemon juice, salt, and white pepper and process until smooth, about 10 seconds, stopping once or twice to scrape the sides. The sauce should have the consistency of mayonnaise.

Transfer the skordalia to a serving bowl and serve as a dip or sauce.

YIELD: 4 TO 6 SERVINGS

# CHAPTER ELEVEN

# Tabletop Companions

WHILE THE RECIPES in *Great Bowls of Fire* are billed as main attractions—the marquee dishes of lunch or dinner—there are a supporting cast of accompaniments that contribute to the pleasures of the table as well. A well-filled bowl is a beautiful thing, but when a condiment, loaf of bread, or grain dish is added, a memorable meal is born.

This chapter offers an entourage of companions for spicy one-pot meals. Soothing condiments such as Cool Cucumber Raita and Coconut-Mint Chutney are ideal toppings for curries, chili-stews, and bean or lentil soups. Chilled beverages such as Horchata and Mango Lassi also complement the electrified palate. In a fix, a dollop of lowfat plain yogurt will often do the trick as a palate soother.

Warm bread makes a natural companion to almost any meal, and many of the recipes throughout *Great Bowls of Fire* suggest serving wholesome breads to soak up flavors. Jalapeño Cheese Corn Bread, Hot Chili Roti, and Roasted Pepper Focaccia are a few breads with a little kick. A variety of breads—whole grain bread, corn bread, and French and Italian loaves—all make desirable companions to spicy one-pot dishes. In addition, ethnic flat breads, such as pita, roti, nan, chapati, focaccia, sopaipilla, and flour tortillas, are great for dipping and scooping. Try them all and try them often.

Rice dishes also make a wonderful bed and side dish for many of the bowls featured in this book. Jasmine, basmati, brown, arborio, white long-grain, Wild Pecan . . . there can never be enough kinds of rice in your pantry. Earthy grains, such as quinoa, couscous, and barley, are also indispensable staples. Rice and grains are perfect for absorbing assertive tastes while providing satisfying sustenance—Yellow Basmati Rice is an excellent example.

# Jessica's Corn Bread

MY FRIEND JESSICA ROBIN not only grows corn on the cob, but after the harvest, she also dries the corn out and grinds it into cornmeal. Her awesome corn bread makes a fitting companion to any bowl of fire.

1 cup yellow cornmeal

1 cup unbleached all-purpose
    flour

⅓ cup sugar

1 tablespoon baking powder

½ teaspoon salt

2 large eggs, beaten

1 cup dairy milk or soy milk

3 tablespoons canola oil

1 can (15 ounces) corn kernels,
    drained

3 to 4 scallions, chopped

2 tablespoons chopped pimientos
    (optional)

PREHEAT THE OVEN to 375 degrees F.
    Combine the cornmeal, flour, sugar, baking powder, and salt in a mixing bowl. In a separate bowl, whisk together the eggs, milk, and oil. Gently fold the liquid ingredients into the dry ingredients until a batter is formed. Fold in the corn, scallions, and optional pimientos.

Pour the batter into a lightly greased 8-inch square baking pan. Bake for 20 to 25 minutes, until the crust is light brown and a toothpick inserted in the center comes out clean. Remove from the heat and let cool for a few minutes. Cut into large pieces and serve warm.

YIELD: 6 TO 8 SERVINGS

# Jalapeño Cheese Corn Bread

A WONDERFUL ACCOMPANIMENT to a bowl of chili, gumbo, or hearty soup.

1 cup yellow cornmeal

1 cup unbleached all-purpose flour

⅓ cup sugar

1 tablespoon baking powder

½ teaspoon salt

2 large eggs, beaten

1 cup whole milk

3 tablespoons canola oil

1 can (11 ounces) corn kernels,
    drained

1 cup shredded cheese (such as Colby
    or Monterey Jack)

2 to 3 tablespoons chopped pickled
    jalapeños

PREHEAT THE OVEN to 375 degrees F.

Combine the cornmeal, flour, sugar, baking powder, and salt in a mixing bowl. In a separate bowl, whisk together the eggs, milk, and oil. Gently fold the liquid ingredients into the dry ingredients until a batter is formed. Fold in the corn, cheese, and pickled jalapeños.

Pour the batter into a lightly greased 8-inch square baking pan. Bake for 20 to 25 minutes, until the crust is light-brown and a toothpick inserted in the center comes out clean. Remove from the heat and let cool for a few minutes. Cut into large pieces and serve warm.

YIELD: 6 TO 8 SERVINGS

# Hot Chili Roti

ROTI IS A flat bread prepared in Caribbean and Indian kitchens. This version is enhanced with jalapeños and cayenne pepper.

| | |
|---|---|
| *4 cups unbleached all-purpose flour* | *½ teaspoon cayenne pepper* |
| *2 teaspoons baking powder* | *½ cup canola oil* |
| *1 teaspoon salt* | *2 tablespoons chopped pickled* |
| *1 teaspoon paprika* | *jalapeños* |

COMBINE THE FLOUR, baking powder, salt, paprika, and cayenne pepper in a mixing bowl. Gradually stir in the oil, 1 cup plus 3 or 4 tablespoons water, and the pickled jalapeños, mixing and kneading the dough with your hands as you go. (Wet your hands if the dough is too dry.) Form a large ball with an elastic texture. Cover the dough with wax paper and set aside for 15 to 30 minutes.

Divide the dough into 6 equal-sized balls. On a waxed or floured surface, flatten each ball and roll out into thin 7-inch flat, round circles. Heat a lightly greased skillet over medium heat and place a round of dough flat in the pan. Cook for 4 to 5 minutes, until the bottom crust is golden-brown. Flip the roti with a spatula and continue cooking until golden-brown. Repeat the process with the remaining dough.

Serve the roti bread with curries, bean soup, chili, and spicy stews and soups.

YIELD: 6 ROTI

# Roasted Pepper Focaccia

HOMEMADE FOCACCIA—a flat, round Italian bread with a chewy crust—makes a delightful accompaniment to soups and stews.

DOUGH

1¾ cups warm water (between 110
    and 115 degrees F)

1 teaspoon active dry yeast

4¼ cups unbleached all-purpose flour

⅓ cup olive oil

2 teaspoons salt

TOPPING

1 cup roasted red peppers, cut into
    strips

3 tablespoons olive oil

2 cloves garlic, minced

2 tablespoons of a mixture of
    chopped fresh herbs (such as
    basil, rosemary, and oregano)

½ teaspoon black pepper

½ teaspoon salt

IN A LARGE mixing bowl, combine the water and yeast. Let stand for about 10 minutes until cloudy and almost foamy. Whisk the liquid until the yeast is completely dissolved.

Gradually mix in the flour, oil, and salt, forming a moist, soft dough. Knead the dough with your hands (or in a dough mixer fitted with a dough hook) for 8 to 10 minutes. Form a large ball and place in a lightly oiled mixing bowl. Coat the dough with the oil by rolling it around in the bowl. Cover the dough with plastic wrap and allow to rise until doubled in bulk, about 2 hours.

Punch down the dough and knead it until it is elastic. Form a large ball and return it to the oiled mixing bowl. Cover with the plastic wrap and let rise a second time until doubled, about 2 hours.

For the topping, in a medium mixing bowl, combine the roasted peppers, 2 tablespoons of the oil, the garlic, herbs, black pepper, and salt. Set aside until the dough is ready to be baked.

Preheat the oven to 400 degrees F. Lightly dust two large baking pans with cornmeal or line with parchment paper. With floured hands, divide the dough into 8 baseball-sized balls. Flatten each ball into a round shape and arrange on the baking pans. Using a spoon, press about 1 tablespoon of topping into the center of each round. With the back of the spoon "brush" the sides of the rounds with the remaining 1 tablespoon of oil. Place the pans in the oven and bake until the focaccias are lightly browned on the bottom, about 20 minutes.

Remove the pans from the oven and allow to cool slightly on a rack before serving.

YIELD: 8 FOCACCIAS

# Jalapeño Biscuits

JALAPEÑOS WILL GO where no chili has gone before. . . .

|  |  |
|---|---|
| 2 cups unbleached all-purpose flour | 1 cup whole milk |
| 2 teaspoons baking powder | 1 tablespoon chopped pickled |
| 1 teaspoon salt | jalapeños |
| ¼ cup margarine or butter | 1 tablespoon canola oil |

PREHEAT THE OVEN to 400 degrees F. Lightly grease a large baking pan. In a medium mixing bowl, combine the flour, baking powder, and salt. With a pastry cutter or your fingers, blend the margarine into the flour mixture until the texture resembles a coarse meal. Stir the milk, pickled jalapeños, and oil into the flour and gently knead until a moist dough is formed, about 30 seconds. (If the dough is too sticky, sprinkle in a little flour.)

With a spoon or melon ball scooper that holds about 2 tablespoons, scoop the dough onto the baking pan. Gently press the dough into round balls while leaving 2 to 3 inches between each drop. Place the pan in the oven and bake for about 12 minutes or until the crusts are light-brown.

Remove from the heat and let cool to room temperature. Store in an air-tight container until ready to serve.

YIELD: 8 BISCUITS

# Yellow Basmati Rice

RICE SOAKS UP the flavors and balances the textures of soups, stews, and curries. So many bowls benefit from a bed of savory yellow rice.

| | |
|---|---|
| 1 tablespoon canola oil | ½ teaspoon turmeric |
| 1 small yellow onion, diced | ½ teaspoon salt |
| 2 cloves garlic, minced | ½ teaspoon white or black |
| 1½ cups basmati rice | pepper |

IN A MEDIUM saucepan, heat the oil over medium heat. Add the onion and garlic and cook, stirring, for 3 to 4 minutes. Stir in 3 cups water, the rice, turmeric, salt, and pepper and bring to a simmer. Cover and cook over medium-low heat until all of the liquid is absorbed, about 15 to 20 minutes. Remove from the heat and fluff the rice. Let stand for 5 to 10 minutes before serving.

Spoon the cooked rice into shallow bowls and ladle the soup, stew, chili, or gumbo over the top.

YIELD: 4 SERVINGS

# Black Bean–Chili Sofrito

SOFRITO IS A versatile condiment of sautéed vegetables, chilies, and herbs. Spoon it over rice dishes, pilafs, burritos, or soups.

1 tablespoon canola oil

1 medium yellow onion, diced

1 green or red bell pepper, seeded and
diced

2 cloves garlic, minced

1 can (15 ounces) black beans,
drained

1 can (14 ounces) stewed tomatoes

2 tablespoons chopped pickled
jalapeños

1 teaspoon dried oregano

½ teaspoon ground cumin

½ teaspoon black pepper

½ teaspoon salt

2 to 3 tablespoons chopped fresh
cilantro

IN A MEDIUM saucepan, heat the oil. Add the onion, bell pepper, and garlic and cook, stirring, for 5 to 6 minutes over medium-high heat. Add the beans, stewed tomatoes, pickled jalapeños, oregano, cumin, black pepper, and salt and cook, stirring, for 7 to 10 minutes over medium-low heat. Stir in the cilantro and transfer to a serving bowl.

Spoon the sofrito over rice, potatoes, squash, or other grain dishes.

YIELD: 6 SERVINGS

### Spice Advice

IF COLORFUL ROCATILLO PEPPERS ARE AVAILABLE, ADD 2 OR 3 (SEEDED AND MINCED) TO THE SIMMERING POT.

# Green Tomato Chutney

HERE'S A GRAND use for the surplus green tomatoes that invade kitchens every autumn.

| | |
|---|---|
| 1 large yellow onion, diced | 3 or 4 cloves garlic, minced |
| 4 or 5 medium green tomatoes, diced | 2 jalapeño or serrano peppers, seeded and minced |
| 4 apples or pears, diced | |
| 1 cup red wine vinegar | 1 teaspoon ground cumin |
| 1 cup apple cider | ½ teaspoon black pepper |
| 1 cup raisins | ½ teaspoon salt |
| ½ cup brown sugar | ¼ teaspoon ground cloves |

COMBINE ALL OF the ingredients in a large saucepan and bring to a simmer. Cook over medium-low heat for about 45 minutes, stirring occasionally. Remove from the heat and let cool to room temperature before serving.

Transfer to serving bowls and serve as a condiment to curries, chicken, or meats. Chill any leftovers. If stored in the refrigerator, the chutney will keep for weeks.

YIELD: 4 CUPS

# Coconut-Mint Chutney

A COOLING CONDIMENT for any curry dish, sambar, or dal.

1 cup shredded coconut
  (unsweetened, if possible)
2 or 3 tablespoons chopped fresh mint
  leaves
2 teaspoons minced ginger root

¾ teaspoon paprika
⅛ teaspoon cayenne pepper
½ cup lowfat plain yogurt
1 teaspoon fresh lemon
  juice

COMBINE ALL OF the ingredients in a mixing bowl and blend well. Chill for 1 hour before serving, allowing the flavors to mingle.

YIELD: 1½ CUPS (4 TO 6 SERVINGS)

# Cool Cucumber Raita

---

RAITA IS A yogurt condiment savored on Indian tables. It complements spicy curries, bean soups, and chili. I like to offer it in place of sour cream when serving black bean soup or chili.

16 ounces lowfat plain yogurt

1 medium cucumber, chopped

2 to 3 tablespoons chopped fresh
mint, basil, or cilantro

COMBINE ALL OF the ingredients in a mixing bowl. Cover and chill until ready to serve.

Serve as a condiment for spicy Indian and Caribbean curries and hearty bean chilies.

YIELD: 2 CUPS (ABOUT 8 SERVINGS)

# Pure Mexican Chili Sauce

THIS POTENT PASTE of pureed dried chilies can be blended into sauces, soups, and stews, or served with burritos, tostadas, or quesadillas.

3 or 4 dried Mexican chilies (such as
    pasilla, ancho, or guajillo)
1 cup simmering water
¼ cup diced yellow onion

1 clove garlic, chopped
½ teaspoon salt
⅛ teaspoon ground
    cloves

REMOVE THE STEMS and seeds from the chilies. Put the chilies in a large ungreased skillet and cook, stirring, over medium heat until lightly toasted, about 2 minutes. Shake the pan and turn the chilies as they cook. Remove from the heat and cover the chilies with the simmering water. Let soak until soft, about 20 minutes. Place a lid or plate over the chilies to keep them from floating.

Add the chilies, ½ cup soaking liquid, the onion, garlic, salt, and cloves to a blender or a food processor fitted with a steel blade. Process until smooth, about 5 seconds. Scrape the pureed mixture into a small bowl.

Add the chili paste to soups, chili, stews, and burritos, or serve as a barbecue sauce.

YIELD: ¾ CUP

### Shopping Tip

A VARIETY OF DRIED CHILI PEPPERS ARE AVAILABLE IN WELL-STOCKED SUPERMARKETS AND MEXICAN GROCERY STORES.

# Scotch Bonnet–Mango Puree

CHILI CONNOISSEURS LOAD their refrigerators with a dizzying array of hot sauces. Others (like myself) take their passion one step further and prepare their own homemade sauces. This fruity and fiery sauce is one of my favorites.

4 to 6 Scotch bonnet peppers, seeded
    and coarsely chopped

1 carrot, peeled and diced

1½ cups apple cider vinegar

1 ripe mango, peeled, pitted, and diced

½ cup diced red onion

Juice of 1 lime

2 cloves garlic, minced

2 tablespoons brown sugar

¼ teaspoon turmeric

PLACE ALL OF the ingredients in a medium saucepan and bring to a simmer over medium heat. Cook for 15 to 20 minutes over medium-low heat, stirring occasionally.

Remove the sauce from the heat and let cool slightly. Ladle into a food processor fitted with a steel blade or into a blender and process until smooth, about 5 seconds. Transfer the sauce to a bowl and serve as a fiery condiment or as a barbecue sauce. Remember to warn your guests before serving.

YIELD: 2 CUPS

# Edible Squash Bowls

---

WHENEVER I REALLY want to impress a guest I'll serve a soup or bisque in the shell of a baked acorn squash. The artful presentation is guaranteed to surprise my guests.

*4 medium acorn squash, rinsed (about 1 pound each)*

PREHEAT THE OVEN to 400 degrees F.

With a sharp knife, cut a round lid off the top of each squash (about 2 inches from the stem). With a sharp-edged spoon, scoop out the seeds and stringy fibers. Cut about ½ inch off the bottom of each squash so that the gourds can stand upright on a flat surface.

Place the squash with their topside down on a baking pan filled with about ¼ inch water. Bake until the flesh is tender, about 25 to 30 minutes. Remove the squash from the oven, flip over, and let cool for 5 to 10 minutes.

Place a squash in the center of each of four bowls. To serve, ladle a soup, chili, or stew into the shell of the squash and serve at once.

YIELD: 4 SERVINGS

# Horchata

---

THIS IS A soothing rice beverage enjoyed throughout Mexico.

*4 cups rice milk*                          *¼ cup honey*
*2 cups cooked white rice*                  *½ teaspoon ground cinnamon*

COMBINE THE RICE milk, rice, honey, and cinnamon in a blender and process until the mixture is smooth (like a milk shake), about 10 seconds. Pour the liquid through a fine sieve and reserve the sweetened liquid.

Fill two glasses with ice and pour the liquid over the top.

YIELD: 2 SERVINGS

---

### Shopping Tip

RICE MILK IS AVAILABLE IN THE

NATURAL FOOD SECTION OF

WELL-STOCKED SUPERMARKETS.

# Mango Lassi

---

THIS IS A cool yogurt beverage popular in Indian cuisine. It makes a soothing companion to spicy curries and other highly seasoned dishes.

It is important to use tender, ripe mangoes, which are much sweeter and more flavorful than hard green mangoes.

| | |
|---|---|
| *1 cup tonic water* | *1 large ripe mango, peeled, pitted,* |
| *1 cup lowfat plain yogurt* | *and diced* |
| *2 tablespoons honey* | *¼ teaspoon ground cinnamon* |

COMBINE THE TONIC water, yogurt, honey, and mango in a blender and process until creamy, about 5 to 10 seconds. Pour into tall cold glasses and sprinkle the cinnamon on top. Serve at once.

YIELD: 2 TO 3 SERVINGS

# Raspberry-Banana Soy Smoothie

---

FRUIT SMOOTHIES MAKE an excellent companion to spicy meals. This healthful version includes soy milk, a nondairy liquid made from processed soy beans.

| | |
|---|---|
| 2 cups soy milk | 2 bananas, sliced |
| 2 cups fresh raspberries or | ¼ cup lowfat plain yogurt |
|    blueberries | ¼ teaspoon ground nutmeg |

COMBINE THE SOY milk, raspberries, bananas, and yogurt in a blender and process until creamy, about 5 to 10 seconds. Pour into cold glasses, sprinkle the nutmeg on top, and serve as a beverage.

YIELD: 2 SERVINGS

### ᵞ¦¦ Shopping Tip

LOOK FOR SOY MILK IN THE NATURAL FOOD SECTION OF WELL-STOCKED SUPERMARKETS, AND OF COURSE, IN ALMOST ANY NATURAL FOOD STORE.

# Index

# More Fabulous Feast Ideas from Jay Solomon

If this is your first Jay Solomon cookbook, there's more where this came from! A celebrated cookbook author and chef with a keen interest in nutrition, Jay has been cooking with flair and entertaining with gusto for more than a decade. His books include:

## *Seven Pillars of Health*

Now you can eat your way to better health—and really enjoy it! The 125 delicious recipes collected here deliver essential nutrition and lip-smacking taste. They include Italian-Braised Rapini with Tomatoes, Banana-Blueberry Bran Bread, Roasted Beet and Potato Salad, and more.

ISBN 0-7615-0862-7 / paperback
368 pages
U.S. $15.00 / Can. $19.95

## *Lean Bean Cuisine*

The world's most perfect protein source stars in this international collection of legumes, peas, lentils, and other beans. More than 100 tasty recipes include Big Lentil Chili, Creole Veggie and Red Bean Jambalaya, Mulligatawny with Chick Peas, and more.

ISBN 1-55958-438-6 / paperback
256 pages
U.S. $12.95 / Can. $17.95

## Vegetarian Soup Cuisine

Gathered around seasonal themes and inspired by international cuisines, these hearty stews, cheerful chowders, and creamy bisques include Spicy Pumpkin and Moroccan Couscous Stew, Mexican Tortilla and Corn Soup, Colorado Anasazi Bean Chili, Gardenfest Gazpacho, and more.

ISBN 0-7615-0190-8 / paperback
288 pages
U.S. $14.95 / Can. $19.95

## Vegetarian Rice Cuisine

These healthful and enticing international rice ideas for breakfast, brunch, dinner, or dessert include Santa Fe Posole Stew, Thai Panang Curry Sauce, Mediterranean Herb and Rice Salad, Chocolate Mocha Rice Delight, and more.

ISBN 0-7615-0081-2 / paperback
224 pages
U.S. $14.95 / Can. $19.95

**Visit us online at www.primapublishing.com**

# To Order Books

Please send me the following items:

| Quantity | Title | Unit Price | Total |
|---|---|---|---|
| _____ | Seven Pillars of Health | $ 15.00 | $ _____ |
| _____ | Lean Bean Cuisine | $ 12.95 | $ _____ |
| _____ | Vegetarian Soup Cuisine | $ 14.95 | $ _____ |
| _____ | Vegetarian Rice Cuisine | $ 14.95 | $ _____ |
| _____ | _____ | $ _____ | $ _____ |

|  |  |
|---|---|
| Subtotal | $ _____ |
| Deduct 10% when ordering 3-5 books | $ _____ |
| 7.25% Sales Tax (CA only) | $ _____ |
| 8.25% Sales Tax (TN only) | $ _____ |
| 5.0% Sales Tax (MD and IN only) | $ _____ |
| 7.0% G.S.T. Tax (Canada only) | $ _____ |
| Shipping and Handling* | $ _____ |
| Total Order | $ _____ |

*Shipping and Handling depend on Subtotal.

| Subtotal | Shipping/Handling |
|---|---|
| $0.00–$14.99 | $3.00 |
| $15.00–$29.99 | $4.00 |
| $30.00–$49.99 | $6.00 |
| $50.00–$99.99 | $10.00 |
| $100.00–$199.99 | $13.50 |
| $200.00+ | Call for Quote |

Foreign and all Priority Request orders:
Call Order Entry department
for price quote at 916-632-4400

This chart represents the total retail price of books only (before applicable discounts are taken).

**By Telephone:** With MC or Visa, call 800-632-8676 or 916-632-4400.
Mon–Fri, 8:30-4:30.

**WWW:** http://www.primapublishing.com

**By Internet E-mail:** sales@primapub.com

**By Mail:** Just fill out the information below and send with your remittance to:

**Prima Publishing
P.O. Box 1260BK
Rocklin, CA 95677**

My name is _____

I live at _____

City _____ State _____ ZIP_____

MC/Visa#_____ Exp. _____

Check/money order enclosed for $_____ Payable to Prima Publishing

Daytime telephone _____

Signature _____